GW00467820

Courageous Conversations

at work

Courageous
Conversations
at work

How to create a
high performing team
where people love to work

LARRY REYNOLDS

Copyright © 2015 Larry Reynolds

The moral right of the author has been asserted.

Apart from any fair dealing for the purposes of research or private study,
or criticism or review, as permitted under the Copyright, Designs and Patents
Act 1988, this publication may only be reproduced, stored or transmitted, in
any form or by any means, with the prior permission in writing of the
publishers, or in the case of reprographic reproduction in accordance with
the terms of licences issued by the Copyright Licensing Agency. Enquiries
concerning reproduction outside those terms should be sent to the publishers.

Matador
9 Priory Business Park,
Wistow Road, Kibworth Beauchamp,
Leicestershire. LE8 0RX
Tel: 0116 279 2299
Email: books@troubador.co.uk
Web: www.troubador.co.uk/matador
Twitter: @matadorbooks

ISBN 978 1784624 293

British Library Cataloguing in Publication Data.
A catalogue record for this book is available from the British Library.

Printed and bound in the UK by TJ International, Padstow, Cornwall
Typeset in 10pt Aldine by Troubador Publishing Ltd, Leicester, UK

Matador is an imprint of Troubador Publishing Ltd

To Monica, Sorcha and Ró

CONTENTS

INTRODUCTION

Your job as a manager is to help your team to deliver great results.

The people in your team will deliver great results if they know what to do, they have the resources to do it, and they want to do it.

It's your job to make this happen.

It sounds simple, but in a world of unique individuals, limited resources and unexpected problems, this can be very challenging.

Unlike the mechanic at your local garage, who has dozens of different tools to fix your car, or a pilot, who has dozens of different controls to land the plane safely, you really have only one tool to get the best out of your team. That's to talk to them. The only way you can create a high performing team is to have good conversations.

Some conversations are easy. You ask someone to do something and they just do it. Some conversations are difficult. What if you ask someone to do something and they ignore you? What if you give a team member some feedback and they get angry, defensive or upset? What if you struggle to motivate someone, however hard you try? What if team members bring you problems to which there are no obvious answers – like a lack of resources?

Just because these conversations feel difficult doesn't mean you should avoid them. In fact, the most difficult conversations are sometimes the most important ones to have. It just takes a bit more courage to have them, and that's why this book is called *Courageous Conversations at Work*.

Over the last 25 years I've worked with over 15,000 managers in a wide range of organisations: big corporations and small businesses, high tech companies and metal bashing manufacturers, pharmaceutical companies, banks and retailers; schools, colleges and universities; hospitals and housing organisations; local and national government; national charities and local arts organisations. The managers who get the best results are the ones that have the best conversations. More specifically, the best managers have six kinds of courageous conversations.

Courageous conversation one - giving and receiving feedback

It's easy to avoid feedback. When someone in your team does something that's not helpful, it's tempting to overlook it and hope things improve of their own accord. After all, you don't want to upset the person, do you? But how will they know what to change if you don't tell them? Great managers give frequent, honest feedback in a way that enhances the relationship. You can find out how they do this in chapter one. Not only do great managers give feedback, they are also experts at requesting feedback and knowing how to act on it.

Courageous conversation two - setting objectives

People can't do a great job unless they know what is expected of them, and have the proper resources to do it. Great managers take the time up front to clarify expectations and make sure the resources are in place. This gives them the right to be uncompromising when it comes to expecting results. Chapter two tells you how.

Courageous conversation three - building trust

One of the most significant differences between managers of high performing teams and managers of low performing teams is the level of trust they engender. In chapter three you will learn about the conversations that help to build trust in your team.

Courageous conversation four - motivation

Are there people in your team who know what to do, and have the skills to do it, but just aren't particularly motivated? Three things affect a person's motivation: the task itself, how much they trust the person asking them, and the way they are asked. Find out how to motivate and engage people in chapter four.

Courageous conversation five - problem solving

You may spend a lot of your time problem solving. But are you sometimes frustrated that your initial solutions don't seem to work, and permanent fixes seem elusive? Great managers get better results because they tend to focus on making robust, measurable progress with a problem, rather than on quick fixes. Find out how in chapter five.

Courageous conversation six - coaching

Coaching your staff has many advantages over just telling them what to do. It leads to higher levels of commitment, better outcomes and develops skills and capabilities. It's also quite difficult to do well, which is why only a few managers ever really master it. If you want to join that group of elite managers who get extraordinary results from coaching staff, then chapter six is for you.

Finally, in chapter seven you can learn how to make a habit of courageous conversations.

Sometimes at work you will use these conversations one at a time. But more often, you will find it useful to switch from one type to another, within a single interaction. You begin a feedback conversation and it becomes clear that the person doesn't know how to do things differently – so you might move into problem solving or coaching to help them. You are doing some problem solving and it becomes clear that the other person doesn't really know what they are meant to be delivering, so you shift to objective setting. The more experienced you become with courageous conversations, the easier it will be for you to switch effortlessly from one approach to another in order to achieve the best outcome.

Some people like to read a book like this all the way through, while others tend to dip in and out to the parts that are most relevant to them at the time. Whatever approach you take, don't just read this book. Put it into action. Use this book to help you have those courageous conversations at work.

If you have more courageous conversations at work the performance of your team will improve, and that's clearly a good thing. But something else rather wonderful will happen too. Your team will enjoy coming to work more. Most people prefer a working environment where people talk to each other in an honest and respectful way, rather than one in which the important things are handled badly or left unsaid. Most of us spend a fair proportion of our time at work, so why not make this time fulfilling as well as productive?

HOW IS YOUR TEAM DOING RIGHT NOW?

Before you start to have courageous conversations with other people, it's useful to have a courageous conversation with yourself. Ask yourself the question, how well is your team doing right now?

You can think of your team members in terms of their skill. How competent are they at doing their job?

You can also think of them in terms of their will. How motivated are they to do their job?

In an ideal world you would probably want all of your team to be highly skilled and highly motivated. I call these people the achievers.

What you don't want is people in your team with no skills and no motivation whatsoever. I call these people the zombies. I hope you don't have any zombies in your team.

You may have people in your team who are high in will but low in skill. They are enthusiastic but not very competent. I call these people the passengers. Sometimes the newest members of your team are passengers. We quite like these people because they are keen to learn, and in most cases, with the right training and development, they will progress to becoming achievers.

More worrying are the people in your team who are highly skilled, but low in will. They know what to do, they just can't be bothered to do it. I call these people the viruses. Like a biological virus, or a computer virus, if you don't tackle them their lack of motivation will infect everyone else.

These definitions are not clear cut. Even your best achievers will have off days when they feel a bit demotivated. Sometimes your passengers can make a huge contribution because they bring a new perspective to the team. Even your worst virus may surprise you with an occasional burst of enthusiasm. But as a framework for helping you to have a courageous conversation with yourself, this model can be useful. If you were to grab a blank sheet of paper and label two sides of a grid, skill and will, where do you think your team members would be right now? Put a cross on your grid to represent your current assessment of each team member's skill and will. You can see an example in figure one.

If all your team members are clustered in the top right-hand corner of the diagram, then either you are already a brilliant manager, you have been very lucky, or you are simply deceiving yourself.

If you have a few passengers, and you have a plan for developing them into achievers, then that's fine.

But if you have a few viruses in the team, or even one or two people in the zombie zone, then bad things happen. In reverse order of badness they are:

Bad thing number three is that your team is almost certainly underperforming, and you don't want to be leading an underperforming team.

Bad thing number two is that it's not much fun for those viruses coming to work each day doing a job that they're not motivated to do.

Bad thing number one is that the achievers notice that the viruses are underperforming. They think it's unfair that the viruses are getting away with it. And the person they blame for this is… you. They stop trusting you and their motivation starts to decline.

If you have people in your team in the virus, passenger or zombie zone, what do you do? You need to have some courageous conversations. In the following chapters of this book you will learn how to have the conversations that can help to create a team of achievers.

Figure 1

Will

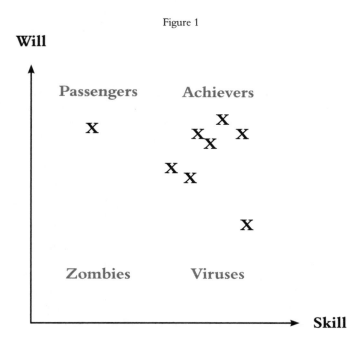

Skill

It's not just about underperformers

Courageous conversations are a powerful tool for managing underperformers. If there are underperformers in your team you should certainly talk to them, probably beginning with a feedback conversation.

But courageous conversations are not just for underperformers.

Here are three reasons why you also need to have courageous conversations with your top performers – the achievers.

Reason number one – the world is changing. Just because someone is highly skilled and highly motivated today doesn't mean that they will stay like that forever. As the world changes, skills become out of date. Unless your achievers keep developing new skills, they will slip back into the passenger category. Your job as manager is to ensure that all your team members keep up to date with the changing requirements of your industry.

People's motivation can change over time too. In fact, some of your present viruses may well have been achievers five or ten years ago. Something's happened to them to reduce their levels of motivation. Don't let that happen to your current achievers. Have frequent courageous conversations with them too.

Reason number two – achievers can deliver more. If you want to create a high performing team, it's just as important to help achievers to deliver even better results as it is to bring underperformers up to an acceptable standard.

Reason number three – you want to retain your high performers. Most people don't leave a job because it's too challenging. Most people leave because it's not challenging enough. If you want to hang on to your achievers, you need to be talking to them about the kind of challenges they need to stay with your team and your organisation. If you don't, they'll be looking for a new job with someone who will.

1. FEEDBACK

Why you need to give feedback

Other people often do things we don't feel entirely happy about. How do you respond?

At work it's often useful to give the person some feedback. Tell them what they've done, point out the consequences, and tell them what you want them to do next time. But giving feedback isn't that easy, for two reasons.

Reason number one is fear. What if the person you are giving feedback to gets really upset? What if they get really angry? What if they stop liking/respecting/trusting you as a result?

Reason number two is time. In a busy working environment, it can be hard to find the right time and place to give feedback.

But if you avoid giving feedback, bad things happen. The person carries on doing things that are unhelpful, your customers get a poor service, and team morale drops. You feel annoyed with them and that's not good for you or your working relationship.

Feedback isn't just about telling people to do things differently. It's also about telling people to continue to do the things they're doing really well. Positive feedback – praise – is just as important as negative feedback – criticism. While positive feedback is just as important as negative, most people find the negative stuff harder to deliver, and that's why we'll focus on it in this chapter.

How to deliver great feedback using E2C2

Before giving feedback you need to make sure that both you and the other person are in a good frame of mind to give and receive feedback. It's often helpful to begin the feedback discussion by saying to the other person, 'I'd like to give you some feedback – is now a good time?'

Assuming they say yes (even a little reluctantly), you begin with the first E.

The first **E** stands for **Evidence**. State, in a neutral tone of voice, what the person has done (or not done). It needs to be objective and factual – so much so that it would stand up in a court of law.

A colleague gives you a report with spelling mistakes in it. Don't say, in an exasperated tone of voice, 'Why are you giving me such shoddy work again?' Do say, in a neutral, professional tone of voice, 'There are spelling mistakes in this report, and here they are.'

The second **E** stands for **Effect.** Explain the effects of what the person has done (or not done).

In this example, you could say, 'When you give me reports with spelling mistakes I feel I need to check them, and that's not a good use of my time.' This explains the effect on you.

You could say, 'If this report goes out with incorrect spelling, that will affect your credibility.' This explains the effect on them.

You could say, 'If this report goes out with incorrect spelling, it will have less credibility because of the spelling mistakes, and that means that the recommendations are less likely to be acted upon. That's not good for our team.' This explains the effect on your team and organisation.

Whether you choose to focus on the effects of the person's actions on you, them, or the team as a whole is a matter of judgment. You may choose to focus on just one or two or all three of these effects, depending on which choice is most likely to get the person to take action.

It's very common to miss out this aspect of feedback, and yet it's critically important. If you miss it out, the person may not realise why they need to change.

C stands for **Continue**. What do you want the person to continue doing as a result of this conversation?

In this example you might say, 'The report itself is really well researched and presented. Please continue to research and present your reports as thoroughly as this.'

C stands for **Change**. What do you want the person to do differently next time? Be as specific as you can.

In this example, you will probably say, 'Make sure the spelling is correct in your next report.'

Although there are two Cs in the E2C2 model, sometimes you only use one of them. If there really isn't anything you want the person to continue doing, just skip to the change bit.

Evidence – 'You've been ten minutes late for work twice this week.'

Effect – 'This means we can't give a good level of service to customers at the start of the working day.'

Change – 'I want you to be on time from now on.'

In this example it would be perverse to make up something under the heading of Continue, just for the sake of it. I've known some managers in this situation who almost fall over themselves to say 'but when you're here you're great, I've no complaints about the actual work, in fact you're one of the best people in the team.' The danger here is that the key message – you need to show up on time – can get lost in a blur of generic niceness. Don't feel that you need to sugar-coat a tough message. If the person needs to change, just say that. If it is appropriate to have both a 'continue' and a 'change' in your feedback, be sure to do it in that order. It's usually easier to continue doing something than it is to change, so make sure that the change bit is at the end where it is most likely to be remembered.

The other time you will use only one of the Cs in the E2C2 model is when you are giving positive feedback.

Evidence – 'That customer was being quite rude and unreasonable towards you, and you really kept calm and professional.'

Effect – 'This prevented the whole thing getting out of hand, and you won the customer over in the end.'

Continue – 'Continue to be as patient and professional with difficult customers.'

Feedback in action

Dawn is an office manager with responsibility for the staff on the reception desk. She has noticed that one of the receptionists, Toby, tends to be quite abrupt to people visiting the building. She decides to talk to him at the end of one of his shifts.

Dawn: Can I talk to you for a couple of minutes?

Toby: OK, what about?

D: I'd like to give you some feedback about how you deal with some of the visitors to the building.

4

T: OK.

D: Is now a good time?

T: As good as any.

D: It's about those two people who came for a meeting with our IT manager. They had to wait a bit, and when you looked up, you didn't say anything – you just raised your eyebrows. When they asked for IT you pushed the visitors' book towards them and said 'sign here' in quite an abrupt tone of voice.

[This is the evidence bit. Although Dawn is tempted to say 'Why were you so rude to those people?' she knows that this would not be helpful – better to describe the behaviour in a neutral tone of voice.]

T: So what's wrong with that?

D: The way people are greeted when they come into the building makes a big difference to our reputation as a company. I want people to feel that we are friendly and professional.

[This is the effect bit.]

T: I am most of the time!

D: You are, Toby – most of the time. Most of the time you are friendly and professional and of course I want you to continue to do that. What I want you to change is to do that consistently, every time – so when people come to the desk, look at them and say 'Good morning, how can I help you?' and smile a bit more. Is that OK?

[Continue and change.]

T: I suppose so.

D: So, to finish, what are you going to take away from this conversation?

T: That I need to be friendly and professional all the time.

D: That's great – thanks.

When and where to give feedback

You should give feedback as soon as possible after the person has done whatever they've done, providing that you've got the right place to do it in, and you are both in a suitable frame of mind.

Let's say that one of your team members is rude in a team meeting and you want to give them some feedback about this. You are not going to deliver that feedback there and then in the team meeting. It's almost never good to criticise people in front of others. Ideally you will give the person that feedback as soon as you can after the meeting, but exactly how, where and when, very much depends on the circumstances. Let's say you find yourself walking away from the meeting together, and you say to them, 'I'd like to give you some feedback about how you came across in that meeting – is now a good time?' If you have a reasonably good working relationship with that person, and you both have a few minutes to spare now, and you are in a place where no one else is listening, that approach will probably work fine. On the other hand, if you have a poor working relationship, or you are feeling quite angry about the outcome of the meeting, and there are lots of other people around, then this approach will probably not work. Much better to leave it for a few minutes until you have calmed down and then arrange to speak to the person later. If you already have a one-to-one meeting scheduled with that person in the next day or two, you may even want to leave it until then, but don't leave it too long. If you don't tell the person for another two weeks they will understandably be a bit miffed that you didn't tell them sooner.

Be mindful about what the person will be doing after you give them the feedback. If you are giving the person some quite tough feedback, do it at a time that allows them to reflect on it a bit afterwards – not just before they are about to give an important presentation, or go into a difficult meeting.

Give feedback in a place where no one else can overhear the conversation. That doesn't mean you need to book a meeting room. It's OK to have a feedback conversation in a communal area, providing you take care not to let other people hear. It's often hard to find a truly private space in an open plan office, so use your judgment about what can be said where. If you give feedback to someone when you are travelling together, think about who else on the train or at the airport might be able to hear your conversation. If you are travelling in a car together make sure the person driving is not distracted by giving or receiving feedback.

As a general rule, you should aim to give feedback little and often. If someone does something – good or bad – tell them as soon as you reasonably can. Frequent informal feedback is much more effective than rare formal feedback. What sort of boss would you rather have – one who gives you lots of feedback throughout the year, or one who saves it all up for a formal annual appraisal meeting?

Getting in the right frame of mind

Have you ever said something when you were feeling stressed or angry and later regretted it? If you have a courageous conversation when you are in the wrong frame of mind then it probably won't go very well. If you want to achieve a good outcome from a courageous conversation you need to be in the right frame of mind.

You want to be feeling purposeful, calm and confident. Here are some practical ways to achieve that, especially if you are feeling a bit cross or stressed.

First of all, take a moment to observe yourself and notice what emotional state you are in. Do you feel angry or stressed or some other strong negative emotion? Noticing your emotions is the first step to managing them.

Secondly, sit as if you are feeling calm and confident. I know this sounds a bit weird, but changing your physiology can change the way you feel. In fact, try this little exercise right now. First sit as you would sit if you were really bored. Even after a few seconds, you'll start to feel a bit more bored than you were before. Now sit as you would sit if you were incredibly alert, interested and curious. After a few seconds you'll start to feel a bit more alert, interested and curious. Now stay sitting like that while you finish reading this book!

Thirdly, think about the purpose of the courageous conversation. What is it that you really want to achieve? If you are feeling especially stressed your initial reaction to this question may be something along the lines of 'I want them to admit to me how horrible they are' or 'I want them to tell me that I am right and they are wrong' or even 'I really want the ground to open up and swallow them so that I never have to deal with them again'. These are not realistic or useful outcomes of a courageous conversation. A more realistic and useful outcome might be 'I want this person to change their behaviour next time'.

There are two benefits to thinking about the purpose of the conversation. Very practically, if you don't know what you want to get out of the conversation, then it's unlikely that you'll achieve it. But thinking about purpose will also help to put you into a better frame of mind. Without going too 'neurosciencey' on you, the bits of the brain that deal with rational thought are different to the bits of the brain that deal with instincts and emotions. Just as strong emotions can get in the way of thinking rationally, so choosing to think rationally can help you to handle strong emotions.

Helping the other person to get in the right frame of mind

You may also need to help the other person to get in a good frame of mind too. If you are initiating the conversation, make sure that you check that the other person is ready. Something along the lines of 'I'd like to talk to you about the ABC project, is now a good time?' or 'I'd like to talk to you about the ABC project, ideally sometime today – when would be best for you?'

Notice your own tone of voice. If you are sounding exasperated, annoyed, patronising or bored, that may put the other person into an unhelpful emotional state. Aim to use a fairly neutral tone of voice. If you are not sure the effect your tone of voice has on other people, then ask them for feedback.

Pay attention to the kind of language you use and the way you introduce the discussion. Choose your words to be relatively neutral. If you begin a feedback conversation by saying 'I have some concerns about…' or 'I am disappointed that you…' then this may trigger some unhelpful emotional states in the other person. Frame the topic more neutrally: 'I'd like to talk about…' or 'I'd like to give you some feedback about…'

FAQ about giving feedback

1. **Does your tone of voice matter?**
   Yes – use a neutral, 'professional' tone of voice. Be respectful of the other person. Do what is genuinely in the best interests of your organisation and the customers you serve.

2. **When should you give the feedback?**
   As soon as possible after the event, providing both you and they are in a good frame of mind. Make sure the person is ready to receive the feedback. Start the conversation with something like: 'I'd like to give you some feedback. Is now a good time?'

3. **Should you use the feedback sandwich?**
   No. In the olden days people were taught to give feedback
   by beginning with a bit of praise, sandwiching in a bit
   of criticism, and finishing with more praise, so that the
   person goes away feeling good.

   It's a terrible way to give feedback. When you give
   another human being a chunk of information they tend to
   remember the stuff at the beginning and the end, not the
   stuff in the middle. So the feedback sandwich structure
   almost guarantees that they won't change. Feedback isn't
   there to help people feel better – it's there to help them do
   their job better.

4. **Is it helpful to ask the person why they were behaving
   in such a way?**
   Usually not, as it puts the focus on the past. The purpose
   of feedback is to get the person to do better in the future.
   A more useful question is, 'What needs to happen for you
   to be able to do it right the next time?'

5. **Is it better to give the person the feedback, or ask
   them first how they think they're doing?**
   This is a theme we'll return to throughout this book –
   when is it better to tell, when is it better to ask? Here's
   how to make that choice when delivering feedback. If the
   person is very self-aware, you have a very positive working
   relationship, and you are pretty sure that they have already
   noticed whatever it is that you want to give feedback on,
   then by all means ask. If they are not so self-aware, or your
   relationship is less than positive, or you are not sure that
   they've noticed, it's better to tell.

   Best to avoid that tricky situation where you say, 'How's
   it going?' through slightly gritted teeth because you know
   it's going badly, and they say, 'Fine, thanks.' You've already
   set yourself up for conflict.

6. **What if the person bursts into tears/flies into a rage/ sulks?**

   Such behaviour is no more acceptable with a colleague than it would be with a customer. Give them time to calm down. Then explain that you would like to be able to discuss things with them in a professional manner.

7. **Can you use the E2C2 approach for anybody?**

   Yes – you can use this approach to give feedback to colleagues, suppliers, customers, bosses, anybody. In fact, some of the most productive courageous conversations may be with your colleagues and boss, as well as with your team members.

   The way you give feedback is exactly the same. Make sure the person is in the right frame of mind, then give the evidence, explain the effects and say what you would like them to continue or change. The big difference is this: when you give feedback to one of your team members, there is a reasonable expectation that they will change – you are their boss, after all. But when you give feedback to your boss, or to a colleague, it's up to them whether they change. In some cases there may be very good reasons why they are doing the things that you'd like them to change. Even if they choose not to change as a result of your feedback, the ensuing conversation can help to improve your working relationship.

8. **What if you don't have the evidence yourself, because another member of staff has complained to you about someone?**

   If you don't have the evidence, you shouldn't give the feedback. It's just not fair to tell someone they're doing something unless you are sure of the evidence. So what if another member of staff complains about a colleague?

   The best course of action is to encourage the complainer to give the person they are complaining about some honest feedback. You can support them in this by teaching them E2C2, helping them plan what to say, and even sitting in on the discussion if that feels appropriate.

If this isn't possible, for example because the complainer is very lacking in confidence, then you need to make sure that what they are saying is accurate. You may need to talk to other staff or customers, or observe the whole team in action. However you do it, you must have the evidence before you give the feedback.

9. **How do you give someone feedback about a poor attitude?**
Sometimes the thing you want the person to change isn't as cut and dried as spelling mistakes in a report or being late for work. Sometimes it's about attitude, style or approach. E2C2 works equally well here. You just have to be a bit more thoughtful about the evidence.

Let's say someone has a bad attitude in team meetings. How do you know? What is it that they are doing that leads you to believe that they have a bad attitude? That's your evidence.

So don't say:

'The evidence is that you have a bad attitude, the effect is that we all hate you and what I want you to change is to have a good attitude.'

Instead, say:

'At the last team meeting, when I began to explain the new shift arrangements, you turned to the person next to you and said, "This is typical, more change for change's sake."

'I found it distracting, and I know other team members found it distracting too.

'What I'd like you to change is this: at the next team meeting, if you want to say something either say it to the whole meeting, or come and talk to me afterwards.'

If the person you have labelled as having a poor attitude is demonstrating all sorts of disruptive behaviours, the chances of getting that person to change all of them at once are small. Better to work on one behaviour at a time.

10. What if I give the person feedback and they don't change?

Most people are creatures of habit, and it takes time to change bad habits into good ones. Give them the feedback again. If they still don't change, say to them: 'This is the third time we're having this conversation. What needs to happen for you to change?'

If they still don't improve you have a decision to make. Are you willing to tolerate this behaviour or not?

If the person generally does their job to a high standard, and there are just one or two areas that you'd like them to change, you may decide that you will tolerate them. After all, nobody's perfect, and sometimes the right thing to do is to accept that the person won't change and instead focus on all the things that the person does well.

On the other hand, if the person is not only failing to improve on the areas that you've given them feedback on, but they are not performing very well at the rest of their job either, then you have a harder decision to make. Are you willing to tolerate this level of performance, or should you remove them from that job?

It's never easy sacking someone, and it shouldn't be. But it shouldn't be completely impossible either.

When people accept a job offer they agree to do some useful things at work in return for being paid some money (possibly not enough money, but that's another conversation). If the person mostly does the right things, then it's right and fair that they get paid to do so. But if the person has stopped doing the right things, and they have been given every opportunity to change, and they still don't change, then it is only right and fair that we stop paying them to do that job.

This may seem harsh, but it is fair. If you work in a private sector company, then your organisation will struggle to keep up with the competition if you are paying your staff to do the wrong things. If you are in the public sector it is wrong to use public money to pay staff to do the wrong things. It's even more wrong that the people your organisation exists to serve – the patients in hospitals, the students in schools, or whoever it is – get a poor service because some of your staff are doing the wrong things.

If you have come to the point where you believe that someone in your team should no longer be working in the organisation, make sure that you discuss it with the relevant people before taking action. The relevant people will usually be your immediate boss, and some kind of Human Resources (HR) person if you have one. If you do decide that you want to sack someone, it must be done in a fair way, both from a legal and from a moral perspective. This often involves using a formal disciplinary or capability procedure. It's beyond the scope of this book to give more detailed advice on how best to use such a procedure, other than to say the more open and honest conversations that take place the better the outcome for everyone concerned.

Continuing the conversation

Sometimes you give the person the feedback, they agree to act on it, and you're done. More commonly however, the feedback is just the beginning of a longer conversation.

How you continue the conversation depends very much on how the person responds. If the person isn't that clear about what you expect them to do, it might turn into a conversation about objectives. If the person knows what to do but doesn't want to do it, it might turn into a conversation about motivation. If the person knows what they should do but doesn't know how to do it, it might turn into a conversation involving problem solving or coaching. We'll look at these different types of conversation in later chapters of this book. But for now, here's a useful framework for continuing the conversation.

A for **Agree**. Say to the person, 'Do you agree with what I've just said?' If your evidence is good, there's a good chance that the person will agree.

If the person agrees that they need to change, it can sometimes be tempting to ask, 'What can I do to help?' Don't do this. You want to encourage the other person to take responsibility for action. So instead of offering to help, move on to:

H for **Happen**. Ask, 'What would need to happen for you to be able to do this?'

Have an honest discussion about what happens next.

How the conversation goes from here depends on how the person is responding. In many cases, if your feedback is accurate, the person will accept that they need to take some action, and you can conclude the conversation by asking:

A for **Action**. Ask the person, 'What will you do as a result of this conversation?' Getting them to say what they will do makes it much more likely that they will take action.

Feedback for evaluation

Most of the feedback you give at work is about specific behaviours and E2C2 is a great tool for doing this.

But occasionally you may give people a different kind of feedback. Instead of focusing on the specific behaviours you want them to continue or change, your feedback evaluates how the person is doing against some agreed standard.

Giving people feedback for evaluation often involves a number somewhere:

- You are in the top quartile (top 25%) of our sales people in terms of overall sales.

- You're doing 70% of the job really well, but you are not really delivering on the other 30%.

- You are at level 3 on the skills matrix for this job.

- You are operating as a 'three star' member of staff this month.

- If there isn't a number, then there's probably some kind of comparison or standard:

- You're below average in the number of invoices you process each day.

- For someone only a few months into this role, you are already performing at a higher level than I'd expect.

- You have passed your technical assessments.

- You have not passed your probationary six months.

One of the most common occasions for giving feedback for evaluation is as part of an annual staff appraisal.

Some appraisals finish with an overall evaluation in words, and some have some kind of numerical scale, for example:

1 – outstanding
2 – very good
3 – acceptable
4 – underperforming

If you need to give someone feedback for evaluation, you need to structure it differently from behavioural feedback. The best way is **standard, rating and evidence**.

Explain as briefly as you can the standard against which you are evaluating this person. Then tell them how you are rating them and why. In a performance appraisal meeting you might say something like this:

'As you know, I have to give you an overall rating based on a scale of 1 to 4. 1 really is outstanding, and is only given to a few people who can demonstrate that they have achieved something really out of the ordinary. 2 is for people who consistently achieve more than their job requires throughout the year. 3 is for people who meet all the requirements of the job and 4 is for people who are underperforming. On that basis I've decided to give you a 2.'

Once you have told the person their rating, you then give them the evidence that led you to that decision. The evidence should be accurate and representative of the whole time period for which the evaluation applies. If it's an annual appraisal, you must have examples from throughout the year, not just the last few weeks. As far as you can, link your examples to the organisational standard, for example:

'You've worked on a number of projects over the year, and with one exception you've delivered them to a high quality, on time and to budget. The one exception was the XYZ project that we've already talked about. Although it went off track and was eventually abandoned, that was partly for reasons outside your control. You did an exceptionally good job on the ABC project. In fact, if next year you turned in three or four projects to the same level as this you'd most likely get the top grade at your appraisal. But for this year, a 2 – very good – is a fair evaluation of what you've actually done.'

For most people, being given a rating is quite a bit of a deal. They may not be able to take in very much else of what you are saying if they are waiting to hear the rating. Their emotional response depends more on what they were expecting to get than on any objective assessment. Someone who expected to get a 1 – outstanding – may be very upset to get only a 2 – very good. Someone who was expecting to get a 4 – underperforming – may be quite pleased to get a 3 – acceptable.

You need to acknowledge that ratings do have an emotional impact on most people and as a result they may not be able to take in very much of what you are saying before the rating (because they are worried about what rating you will give them) or after the rating (because they are dealing with the emotional impact, good or bad, of having heard what it is). So be mindful of this if you need to have a longer conversation before or after delivering the rating.

Most people feel passionately about fairness. That's why it's so important to explain both the standard and the evidence when you are giving someone feedback for evaluation. If you do this well, they will feel fairly treated. If you skip either step or do it shoddily, they may feel unfairly treated both by the system and by you.

When to give feedback for evaluation

Feedback about behaviour is important and useful. It's only when you give people specific examples of what they need to continue doing and what they need to change, that performance and job satisfaction improves.

Feedback for evaluation is more problematic. Saying to someone, 'Your rating this year is a 2' is not very helpful if they don't know what they need to do to get a 1 next year. Sometimes a low rating can motivate people to improve. But it can also make people resentful and mistrustful of the whole rating system.

However, there are three specific circumstances where you might find it useful to give feedback about overall performance

1. **Formal appraisal schemes**

    Your organisation may require you to give feedback for evaluation as part of an annual, six-monthly or quarterly appraisal. If you have to do this then do it well, using the standard, rating, evidence approach. Be sure to accompany it with plenty of feedback about behaviour so that the person knows what they need to do to maintain or improve on their current rating.

2. **People who are new, inexperienced or lacking in confidence**

    Sometimes you give someone feedback about behaviour, but they interpret it as feedback for evaluation. For example, you might say to a new member of staff, 'The way you are entering the data means it doesn't get saved properly, so what I would like you to change is…'

    What you are intending to communicate is a simple tip for doing the job better. But if that person is new, inexperienced, or lacking in confidence, they may interpret it differently. The message they hear is 'I'm really terrible at this job because my boss is criticising me again'. In other words, although you are giving specific feedback about behaviour, they are interpreting it as feedback for evaluation.

    If you think this is likely to happen, it can be useful to nip it in the bud by giving some feedback for evaluation just before you give the specific feedback for behaviour, like this:

'Given that you've only been in your new role for three weeks, you are doing very well overall. There's something I want to show you to help you do it even better and it's this. The way you enter data doesn't get recorded properly…'

3. **When people ask you for it**
   Sometimes people ask you for feedback for evaluation. They want to know how well they are doing. If they ask for this kind of feedback, prepare it carefully and give them the information they need.

Receiving feedback

There are three reasons why you should actively encourage the people you work with to give you feedback.

Firstly, it helps you to do your job better.

Secondly, it helps to build trust with your colleagues.

Thirdly, it will encourage them to be more open to the feedback you want to give them.

Despite this, most people find it difficult to ask other people for feedback. There's a paradox at the heart of being a human being; on the one hand we want to learn, develop and grow (so give me lots of critical feedback to help me do this), and on the other hand we want to be accepted as just fine as we are (so if you must give me feedback, make sure it's all positive).

The most common response to *critical* feedback is to be defensive, to come up with reasons why you had to act in that way. The most common response to *positive* feedback is to brush it off with comments like 'It was nothing' or 'You'd have done the same yourself'. Neither of these responses is helpful. For feedback to be useful, you have to listen to it and respond productively. Here's how.

Listen

When someone gives you some feedback, listen to what they have to say. Don't interrupt to tell them they're wrong. Don't look impatient and angry. Don't check your emails on your smartphone. Just listen. Even if they don't seem to be expressing themselves that well, imagine that buried inside that mass of words is some really useful information – because there almost certainly is.

Probe

Most people are not very good at giving feedback, and they may well express it in rather vague and unhelpful terms. Probe for more detail. Ask questions like:

- What specifically did I do?
- Why is this important?
- How exactly would you like me to do this next time?

By probing in this way you are helping the person giving the feedback to give you high quality information under the headings of Evidence (What specifically did I do?), Effect (Why is this important?), Continue and Change (How exactly would you like me to do this next time?)

Respond

There are three useful ways of responding to feedback. Being defensive isn't one of them.

Number one is to agree to take action. If what the person says makes sense, and it feels right to do so, agree to do what they are suggesting.

Number two is to thank the person for their feedback, saying no to whatever they are suggesting and telling them why.

How is the latter different from being defensive? Saying no is future focused – 'I won't be doing as you suggest because…' Being defensive is past focused – 'I did this because…' How defensive you come across to the other person also depends on your tone of voice.

Number three is to tell the person that you need time to think about what they have said. This is an especially useful response when you can see why the person wants you to behave in a certain way, but it's just not feasible for you to be able to do that. Once you've had time to think, get back to the person, acknowledge their perspective, tell them why you can't do exactly what they want, and engage in some problem solving to meet their needs in a more creative way.

Receiving feedback in action

Liam is a manager and Ryan is a newish member of his team. They are having a one-to-one meeting at Ryan's request.

L: You wanted to give me some feedback?

R: Yes, thanks for making time to see me. It's just that I don't feel I'm getting as much support from you as I would like.

[A defensive response to this comment would be something along the lines of: 'Well, Ryan, you have to understand that I'm very busy, and anyway I would expect someone like you not to need much support.' Instead Liam listens and probes for some examples.]

L: What kind of support do you need?

R: Well, when you give me a project I'm pretty much left to myself to do it in my own way. It would be good if you just asked me now and again, 'How's it going?' – then at least I'd know that you were interested.

L: OK… just tell me a bit more about why this is important to you. Are you getting stuck sometimes with the project and don't know what to do or is it more about reassurance, knowing that you're doing the right thing?

R: It's a bit of both really – I suppose if I get stuck I can always ask Eleanor [a more experienced team member] but I don't think you always appreciate what I do.

L: Well, first of all thanks for the feedback. It's not always easy giving straight feedback to your boss. I'd love to have the time to be asking you 'How's it going?' on a more frequent basis, but I'll be honest with you and say that that's not going to happen – I just have too much on my plate. However, if you're not sure about how to proceed, and Eleanor isn't available or can't help, do feel free to ask me and I'll respond as soon as I can.

As for the bit about appreciating what you do, I have been guilty of not expressing that clearly enough. You've only been here – what, six months? – and I think you've made a really excellent start. I'll commit now to expressing my appreciation more clearly in future – assuming of course that you continue to do great work! – and I'll do that when we review each project on completion. How does that sound?

R: Sounds good – I appreciate you taking time to listen to me.

2. OBJECTIVES

Why you need to set objectives

Organisations exist to get things done. If your organisation is going to provide a good service to its customers, everyone who works for the organisation has to know what they must do to make this happen. In other words, everyone has to have clear objectives.

Objectives come at different levels. Most people have annual objectives and maybe quarterly objectives as well. Some people in your organisation may be responsible for projects – chunks of work that take weeks or months to deliver. And then there are tasks that take minutes or hours to complete. The clearer people are about what is expected of them, the better they will perform and the happier your customers will be.

There's also the psychological benefit of clear objectives. People who are clear about what they are expected to achieve on a daily, weekly, monthly and annual basis tend to be more engaged at work. Clear objectives not only lead to high performing organisations, they also help to create organisations where people love to work.

That's why one of your key tasks as a manager is to make sure that every person in your team has clear objectives. This is not an easy task. How do you make sure that every team member understands what is expected of them? How do you make sure that they are motivated to do it? How do you make sure that they actually deliver?

How to set objectives with OPERA

O stands for **Objective** – what you want the person to do.

This may be a very specific task, such as booking a meeting room. It may be a huge project such as implementing a new IT system for your organisation. Begin with a short, high level summary of what you want the person to do.

P stands for **Parameters** – how you will measure that the task has been done to the standard required. This is sometimes known as the measure of success, or 'what good looks like'.

In the case of a simple task, the parameters may be quite concise. For example, 'We need a meeting room that can hold 12 people and has access to conference calling facilities.' In the case of a bigger project, there may be quite a list of things, but the principles are exactly the same.

E stands for **Effects** – what are the effects of doing, or not doing this task? Why does this task need to be done?

Every day, in thousands of organisations all over the world, bosses give their people tasks to do, and forget to spell out why the task is important. As a result, the person lumbered with the task doesn't feel very motivated to do it, and they may not do it well, or even at all. It's not that they sit twiddling their thumbs – most people work pretty hard – they just find something more interesting, more worthwhile to do. This is especially true if you are asking your team member to follow some procedure that the team member can't really see the point of.

But if you explain the effects of doing – or not doing – the task, this can help to motivate the person to do it and do it well. It's often more effective to explain the bad things that might happen if the task is not done, than to explain the good things that will happen if it is done. Telling someone, 'One of our operators was once seriously injured because he failed to follow the correct procedure' is usually more effective than saying, 'If you follow this procedure we will score well when the auditors come round.'

If you do want to motivate people by talking about the negative consequences of not doing something, these must be genuine consequences, not threats. 'Someone was once seriously injured because he failed to follow the procedure' is a genuine consequence. 'If you don't follow the procedure I'll have to think very carefully about your long-term future with this company' sounds more like a threat.

R stands for **Resources.** Doing any task, big or small, requires resources – equipment, materials, information, access to people, etc. If you don't ensure that the resources are in place, the person will almost certainly fail. Although the resources needed will depend very much on the nature of the task or project, there's one resource that's always needed and always limited – time.

When you are asking someone to do something, it's a good idea to ask, 'How much time will you spend on this?' This isn't the same as 'When will it be done by?' We'll come to that in a moment when we talk about accountability. It's about the number of hours that the person will spend on that task or project.

There are at least three reasons why it's good to ask the question, 'How much of your time will you spend on this?'

Firstly, it helps to make sure that you and the team member have a shared view of the scale of the task. To some extent you will have covered this in the Parameters part of the discussion, but if you expect a report to be written in an hour, and they expect to spend a whole day on it, then further discussion is needed.

Secondly, it helps avoid the most common reason why things don't get done – lack of time. Unlike most other resources, time is strictly limited. There are only ever 24 hours in the day, 168 hours in the week, and few of us want to spend all of this working. Having a realistic idea of how long a task will take before committing to it makes it much more likely the task will get done.

Thirdly, it gives you the right to hold the person accountable.

A stands for **Accountability**. By when will it be done? A simple task will have a simple final deadline. A more complex project may have a series of milestones along the way. Make sure the person knows that they are not only responsible for achieving the objective, but also that they are responsible for letting you know when they have done so. And, in the event that they think they will miss the agreed deadline, it's also their responsibility to let you know *before the deadline has passed*.

OPERA in action

Duncan is head of organisational development (OD) for a national retailer, and Ann is an OD adviser. They are meeting to discuss a new project.

D: I'd like you to take on a new project and it's to redesign our performance appraisal system for store managers. We've been using the same paper-based approach for quite a few years now, and no one seems to like it much. It's time for a revamp, and I'd like you to lead on this. [Objective]

A: OK, when do you want it by?

D: We'll come on to that in a minute. First I want us to be clear about what the new performance appraisal needs to be able to do. I've got three key criteria in mind. First, everyone needs to do it – at the moment about one in four store managers don't even get an annual appraisal. Secondly, it must be accessible online, not paper based. And thirdly, it must lead to better performing store managers. [Parameters]

A: If we're going for an online system it'll be easy to measure compliance rates. I agree with you that it needs to improve performance, otherwise what's the point? That'll need more thought. Can I ask why we're doing this and why now?

D: It's a combination of reasons. The trading climate is still very tough for us so our CEO is keen to pull any levers he can to improve performance. Plus ever since I came here just over a year ago I've been concerned that the current appraisal process doesn't really deliver anything useful. [Effects]

A: Makes sense.

D: I'd like to give you a sense of the scale of this project. I imagine that you will spend one or two days a week on this for the next three months, and that will give you enough time to come up with a pilot that we can test in one of the regions. After that it's tweaking the system and rolling it out across all the stores. You'll probably want to put together a small project team including a store manager, an area manager and maybe someone from HR. [Resources]

A: OK, that makes sense too, although to be honest that sounds quite a tight timescale.

D: Yes, maybe it is. Ideally the new system would be rolled out in December [Accountability], but I guess you won't know really what's realistic until you get stuck in. Here's my suggestion for how you begin. Feel free to ask me any other questions you have now, and then go away and draw up a short project plan for how you would go about it. Let's meet next week to talk through the plan and we'll see where we go from there.

A: Sounds perfect – I'll get cracking. I do like the idea of piloting something before we roll it out across the company, but I'm not sure that putting together a project team in the way you suggest is necessarily the best way forward. Are you open to other approaches providing I deliver the same end goal?

D: Yes, I'm very open to other ideas – as you say, what matters is achieving the end goal. Also, as well as drawing up a plan for this project, can you put together some ideas on how we might measure how a new appraisal system can actually improve performance? Without that, you might spend a lot of time doing something that's not really worthwhile.

A: I'll do that.

What not to say when setting objectives

When you are setting objectives it's very important to discuss what the objective is (Objective and Parameters), why it's important (Effects), the resources needed (Resources) and when it needs to be delivered by (Accountability). But as far as possible, you want to avoid telling the person in much detail **how** they will complete the task. Why? Because the more you specify how the person is to complete the task, the less responsibility they will feel for it. Not only will they feel more responsible if you let them do it their way, they will probably do a better job too.

Sometimes it's very easy to avoid telling the person how to do the task. If you are asking an experienced colleague to book a meeting room, you probably don't need to tell them how to do it.

But what if the person is very inexperienced, and really doesn't know how to do the task that you are setting them? In this situation, while it sometimes makes sense for you to tell them how to do it, don't ignore the other options – like asking them to find out for themselves.

With more complex tasks, you may be tempted to tell the person how to do it, simply because you have more experience. That's fine, provided you make it clear that the other person is free to ignore your advice if they can come up with a more effective way of meeting the objective. In the example above, Duncan made two suggestions about how the objective was to be achieved – doing some piloting and setting up a project team. But he was happy for Ann to ignore these suggestions if she could find another way to deliver the end goal.

When and where to set objectives using OPERA

You can use OPERA whenever you are asking another person to do something, whether it's a simple task, a complex project, or anything in between. Exactly how you use it depends on the person you are asking to do the task, their level of competence and commitment, and the relationship you have with them.

Although OPERA is a particularly useful tool to make sure that your team members are clear about the goals you expect them to achieve, it can also be useful when someone gives you work to do. Have you ever been in a situation where your boss or another senior person gives you a task to do 'as soon as possible', without clear guidance on exactly what is required, why it's important, or how long you are expected to spend on it?

Instead of agreeing immediately to do what you think your boss wants you to do, use OPERA as a checklist for asking some useful questions. What does good look like for this task? (Parameters) Why is it important? (Effect) How long do you expect me to spend on this? (Resources) When do you need it done by? (Accountability) Taking this approach will not only make you appear more professional, but it may also make your boss think twice about routinely dumping stuff on you.

You can also use OPERA to plan out your own work, especially if you are taking on a complicated project.

FAQ about objective setting

1. **What's the difference between objectives, goals, targets and outcomes?**
   Some people might try to make a distinction between these various terms, others regard them as essentially the same. Take your pick.

2. **What about SMART goals?**
   This won't be the first time you've learnt about goal setting. In fact, there's a pretty good chance that at some time you've been taught to set SMART goals. Goals should be Specific, Measurable, Achievable, Realistic and Time-related.

   The problem with SMART is that it's a bit confusing (How is specific different to measurable? Isn't achievable and realistic the same thing?), and it misses out a very important element of effective goal setting, which is the discussion about resources. That's why OPERA is better. OPERA is defined in the Oxford English dictionary as 'dramatic performance', and if you use OPERA well at work, that's what you will get.

3. **Do you always have to cover all five parts of OPERA?**
   OPERA is a checklist you can use to make sure that you and the other person have a genuinely shared view of the task that needs to be done. You don't have to cover every one of the five areas if that understanding already exists. If you ask someone to book a meeting room you probably don't need to spell out the effects or the resources – unless of course they are new and don't know how to access your organisation's online room booking system.

4. **Should you use OPERA to tell the person what to do, or should you ask for their views?**
   With a less experienced team member, and more straightforward tasks, it probably makes sense to tell; with

a more experienced team member, and more complex projects, it probably makes sense to ask for their opinion. Quite often objective-setting conversations are a mixture of telling and asking, as in the example of Duncan and Ann above.

5. **What about competing objectives?**
   OPERA is a great tool for setting a specific objective, large or small. But objectives don't exist in isolation. A person's ability to deliver objective A depends on how much time they have already committed to objectives B, C and D.

   The best way to handle this is during the Resources part of the OPERA discussion, and in particular the question 'How much time will you spend on this?' Once the person has given their reply, the natural follow-up questions are 'Have you got this time available before the final deadline?' and 'If not, what are you going to do about this?' There are no simple answers to these questions, but asking them before the person begins to tackle the objective is generally much better than waiting for them to discover halfway through that they really don't have the time to do this.

   If the person feels that they don't have the time to deliver all the objectives for which they are responsible, it may be useful to have a problem solving or coaching conversation with them, using some of the tools from later in this book.

6. **What if the person doesn't deliver?**
   Tell them. Use E2C2 to give them feedback.

7. **Can you use OPERA to set team objectives as well as individual ones?**
   Yes.

Creating a culture of delivery

You ask one of your team members to do a piece of work. They agree to do it. Time passes. The deadline passes without any sign they've done it. You chase them. They say, 'Sorry, I was too busy.'

Has this ever happened to you? Almost certainly, because it happens every day in thousands of organisations around the world. How do you respond? Do you say, 'I know we're all busy, but can you try and do it as soon as possible?' or do you say, 'That's not acceptable – when one of my team members agrees to do something, I expect them to deliver'? In other words, are you basically forgiving or are you uncompromising? Would you like to be forgiving or would you like to be uncompromising?

Over recent years I've taken to asking managers on my Courageous Conversations training courses how much of their time they spend chasing people who've failed to do the things they've said they would do. The amount of time varies wildly, from about 10% to about 90%, with an average of about 20%. So if this rough and ready poll is in any way representative, on average, managers in the UK waste a day a week chasing people for work they should have done in the first place. Just think how much more productive our hospitals, schools, government and businesses could be if managers didn't have to waste time chasing.

So how do you go about creating a culture of delivery in your organisation – a culture where people do what they agree to do, without the need for chasing? You need to be uncompromising when it comes to holding people accountable for delivering results. I'm not advocating a completely ruthless approach to management. Sometimes people fail to deliver because of a genuine emergency. If one of your team members says, 'I didn't complete that report because my daughter broke her arm and I had to take her to hospital' you are not going to be uncompromising then. I hope you will be humane, ask after the welfare of the child, and reschedule the work. But such genuine emergencies are comparatively rare. If your team member merely says 'I was just too busy' then you need to be uncompromising.

But you only earn the right to be uncompromising if you have made sure that the person taking on the task really understands what is involved, why it's important, and has the resources to deliver. That's why the OPERA checklist is so important.

Objective setting and flexible working

Once upon a time going to work meant just that. People came to an office or factory or shop in the morning, and worked until it was time to go home. Managers were usually in the same physical location as the staff they supervised, and provided staff looked busy, managers were generally pretty happy.

That's no longer the case. Hardly anyone these days goes to the same place every day and works a standard 9–5 day. Most people work flexibly in some way: flexible times, flexible locations, or both. Most likely at least some of the people in your team work at different times, or in a different place to you. If you can't be there to see what they are up to and to help them when they get stuck, it's even more important that they have clear, well-resourced objectives. As flexible working becomes more common, it will be even more important for managers to be able to set very clear expectations, and hold people accountable for achieving them.

3. TRUST

Why you need to build trust

You may think that if you are the boss your people ought to do what you tell them to do. Back in the twentieth century this may have been true, but in the twenty-first century formal authority can only take you so far. In the modern workplace, getting things done depends less on formal authority and more on relationships of trust. If I ask you to do something, and you trust me, you are much more likely to do the task and do it well. Relationships have always been important in business, but never more so than now.

It takes time to build a relationship of trust. To a large extent people will trust you based on what you do rather than what you say. But there are some very specific things you can do to accelerate the trust building process, and the most important thing is to have the right kind of conversation.

There are two kinds of work conversation. There are conversations about getting things done, and there are conversations about relationships. If you say to someone, 'What time is the delivery due?' then that's a conversation about getting things done. But if you say to someone, 'We've just been assigned as joint leads on this new project – how should we best communicate with each other?' then this is a conversation about relationships.

Although good relationships are an essential foundation for getting the work done, we often fail to spend enough time on them – unless something goes horribly wrong, in which case we are sometimes forced to have the conversation.

In this chapter I'm going to suggest that you spend some time having some relationship building conversations – specifically some conversations about building trust.

There are degrees of trust. It's not a question of whether you trust someone or not – it's more a question of how much you trust them and in what circumstances.

How to have trust building conversations

Level one – factual stuff

Relationships begin with knowing some basic facts about the other person. If you already know some basic facts about the people in your team – previous jobs, family, and interests outside work – then you can skip this conversation and move on to level two. But if you don't then you really need to find out. Here are some useful questions to ask them:

1. Where were you brought up?
2. What did you do before this job? (study, parenting, travel, other jobs)
3. Where do you live now?
4. Who are the other people in your immediate family? What do they do?
5. What interests do you have outside work? (hobbies, sports, travel, community, friends)

Unlike giving feedback and agreeing objectives, where there is a definite template for your conversation – E2C2 and OPERA respectively – there is no single structure for trust building conversations. You can use the questions I suggest as a starter for the conversation. Be genuinely curious and interested in the other person and ask whatever questions seem appropriate. If the person seems keen to tell you more, listen carefully. If the person seems unwilling to talk about a particular aspect of their lives, respect that and move the conversation on. It's not an interview – it's a conversation.

Be ready to tell them a bit about your circumstances too if it feels right to do so.

It's obviously easier to ask these questions if the person hasn't been a member of your team for very long. It would feel a bit strange suddenly asking them if you've been working with the person for years. But if you have been working with someone for a long time and you don't know the answers to most of these questions, you're unlikely to build much trust with them until you do.

Level two – preferences and values

The next step up in building trust is to move on from questions of fact to questions about preferences and values. You may already have found yourself doing this in the previous conversation, but if not, now's the time. A good way to start this conversation is to ask:

1. What do you like about your present job?
2. What do you not like about your present job?

Listen carefully and be curious. Encourage the person to give examples and tell you more. If they say, 'The pressure I'm under', ask them, 'What's the most pressured thing about your job? What's one change that would make it less pressured? Is the pressure all bad?'

This conversation can lead to at least three good things:

First, the relationship gets better, because the other person feels that you are taking a genuine interest in them.

Secondly, you're starting to learn what makes this person tick. This information is really useful when it comes to motivating them.

Thirdly, and perhaps surprisingly, it can help the person to be more committed to their job. Why? Because it will help them to be clearer for themselves about what their preferences and values are. People who are clear about their own preferences and values tend to be more highly committed to their work than people who are not.

Level three – seeking feedback

You've learnt some basic facts about the person, and you've learnt a bit about their preferences and values at work. Now you need to get a bit more personal by asking them about the impact you have on them as a manager. It's time for you to ask them for some feedback.

Here are some useful questions to ask:

1. What do I do as your manager that helps you do your job well?
2. What do I do as your manager that gets in the way of you doing your job well?
3. What could I do to help you do a better job?
4. What could I do to help you enjoy your job more?

If the person seems a bit critical of you as a manager, don't be defensive, and don't think you have to change immediately. The most important thing is to listen. Then you can respond, either by changing some of the things you do, or by explaining why you will not be changing. (There's more on this listen, probe, respond approach in the receiving feedback section of chapter one.)

If you do this conversation well, two good things happen. The person trusts you more, because they feel that you are genuinely interested in what they think and you learn some useful information about what you can do to be a better manager.

There's one more question you can ask, if you feel courageous enough to do so. It is:

5. What do I need to do as a manager to demonstrate that you can trust me?

Almost every human being values trust and wants to spend time with people they trust. But people can have different ideas of what trust is. You may think that being open and honest is one of the most important things, but that won't necessarily increase trust with someone who considers reliability to be key. The best way to find out which aspects of trust the other person considers important is to ask them. Most definitions of trust fall into four main areas:

Competence – do you know what you are doing? Do you have the skills to do your job, and the knowledge about what's going on in your team, department, organisation and industry?

Openness – do you communicate openly and honestly with your team?

Reliability – do you deliver on your promises? Do you act in a consistent way?

Kindness – do you care about the other person? Do you take their feelings into account?

Although all four areas are important to almost everyone, most people care more about some than others. When you ask people what you need to do to be a good manager, and they say something along the lines of: 'I need you to set out a clear view of where we're going as a department, and prove to me that we can achieve it', then that person probably has competence and reliability high on their list. On the other hand, someone who replies to the same question with, 'Communication is really important – you have to make sure that you let me know what's going on and that you listen to what I have to say', probably values openness and kindness more.

It's not easy to create high levels of trust at work. But if you can demonstrate your competence, communicate openly and honestly, keep your promises (and hold others accountable for theirs) and show that you care about others, you've got a pretty good chance.

Level four – being vulnerable

If you've got to know the people you work with, and have discovered something of their preferences and values, and have learnt what you need to do to be a great manager, then you've probably already created some quite high levels of trust. But if you want to create the very highest levels of trust, you have to be willing to show your vulnerability.

On your first day at work you probably felt fine asking lots of questions and admitting all the things you didn't know. But as you progress to more senior levels of management, the temptation to present huge confidence to the rest of the world can be very strong. The higher up the organisational hierarchy you go, the harder it is to show your vulnerability.

One of the many paradoxes of being a human being is that when we're in these management and leadership roles, we are often tempted to appear super confident and all-knowing. We assert confidently that we know the answers to questions. We insist that we are on the right course of action to achieve the desired goals. And if we do make mistakes, we justify our actions by blaming others. But the more we act this way the less trustworthy we appear. Who do you trust most – the person who claims they know all the answers and never admits to mistakes, or the person who sometimes admits they don't know and who apologises when they've done the wrong thing?

Of course there's a balance to be struck here. If you never seem to have the answers to any problem, and are apologising all the time because you blunder from one mishap to another, then that won't create much trust. People will just think you're incompetent. But it's just as bad to go too far the other way – if you never make mistakes, and always appear to know the answer to every problem then that won't create much trust either.

So how do you get the balance right? Only you can say. You certainly need to know the right answers and make the right decisions most of the time, but when you don't, you need to be very open about it. Here are three conversations you might need to have which are about showing your vulnerability. One is about how to say 'I don't know', one is about how to say 'I'm sorry', and one is about sharing personal information.

How to say 'I don't know'

When you are faced with a problem or challenge and you don't know the answer, simply pretending that you know the solution is not a good thing to do. But it's almost as bad to say 'I don't know', shrug your shoulders and walk away. These steps can help.

First acknowledge honestly the parts of the problem you do understand and the parts you don't. Quite often you know what's currently happening and how you would like things to be, you just don't know the best way to get there. If that's the case, acknowledge that honestly.

Secondly, for the things you don't know, ask the question, 'What do we need to do to find out?' This might involve further research, or a bit of trial and error. It might mean more data gathering about the problem. It might involve a different set of people in the problem solving activity. Posing the question, 'What do we need to do to find out?' is not only extremely useful in itself, but it greatly enhances your credibility as a person who doesn't rush into simplistic solutions for complex problems.

How to say 'I'm sorry'

Simply saying, 'Sorry, let's move on,' isn't enough. A proper apology follows these three steps.

1. Use specifics. Instead of just 'Sorry', say, 'Sorry I had to cancel our meeting at short notice.'

2. Acknowledge the other person's feelings – 'It is very frustrating when you get messed around, especially when you're really busy.'

3. Show that you are committed to change – 'As well as rescheduling this meeting, I'd like to get all our meetings for this project in the diary now, so that I can schedule my other stuff around it.'

Obviously you can go too far. Too much grovelling won't do your credibility any good at all. But doing these three small things is usually a lot better than just saying sorry.

Sharing your personal history

There's another way to be more vulnerable and that's by sharing some aspects of your personal life and history. In a sense this brings us back full circle to the level one conversation about factual stuff, but at a deeper level.

I was once asked to deliver a keynote address at a conference for a property company. This company owned a substantial portfolio of properties across the company, but relied on independent managing agents to handle the day-to-day maintenance and administration of these very diverse properties. This was the first time the property company had arranged such a conference, and it was a very big deal for them. As well as my keynote speech, the MD was due to do a big piece on the company's strategy for the year ahead and what it meant for the managing agents.

A few weeks before the conference the MD announced that he was asking his deputy to deliver the strategy slot. He would try to pop in on the conference if he could, but would probably miss most of it. His team were amazed at this decision but as the MD had a reputation for being remote and autocratic, no one felt able to ask why.

On the morning of the conference itself, the managing agents were none too pleased either to discover that the MD wouldn't be there to deliver his strategy slot.

But when it came to the strategy session, the MD was there and he took the stage. Instead of the usual dull PowerPoint slide, behind him on the screen was a holiday snap of the MD, his wife and three boys.

The MD began. 'I'm sorry that I can't stay to deliver the strategy presentation you were expecting. My youngest son has autism and today is his first day at secondary school. As some of you may know, children with autism often have a lot of difficulty adapting to a new routine, and for my son, moving to a new school is a massive change of routine. When I discovered that we'd arranged this conference on the same day that my son was starting his new school, I decided that I needed to be there to support him. That's where I've been this morning and I'll be going back there in a few minutes. I'm sorry not to be with you, but my deputy Ian has been closely involved in developing the strategy and he'll do a brilliant job of explaining it – better than me, probably. So thank you for listening to me, enjoy the rest of the conference, and I look forward to spending more time with you next time we meet.'

In the few minutes that it took to say those words, the MD's reputation and trustworthiness in the eyes of both his staff and the managing agents changed hugely for the better. The right degree of sharing can have a big positive impact on the extent to which people will trust you.

How much do you choose to share with the people you work with? Again, only you can say. Too much personal detail too soon can be embarrassing and counterproductive. But too little can give the impression that you don't really care. Think carefully about what to share, with whom, and when.

When and where to have trust building conversations

Trust building conversations should be fairly informal. If you said to a member of your team that you'd like to meet with them for an hour at 3pm to have a trust building conversation, that would be a bit weird. The informal stuff works best. You may find yourself on a car journey with a colleague you don't know so well, and naturally you get chatting about where you live, and what you like to do outside work. After a bit you might get chatting about your current jobs, what you like and what you don't like. This naturally leads on to a conversation about what your bosses do that makes life easier or more difficult for you both, and this might lead on to a conversation about how difficult it is to do a job well, with a bit of mutual sharing about mistakes you have both made in the past, and things you are struggling with right now. Without even thinking about it consciously, you have had a series of trust building conversations at the four levels of factual stuff, preferences and values, what you want from your manager and showing vulnerability. If you've ever had this kind of car journey with a colleague, or this sequence of conversations in any context, you will know how powerful it is in building trust. You feel differently about the person – and they feel differently about you – at the end of it.

If you have worked with your team for some time, you may well have had these kinds of trust building conversations quite naturally, without having to think much about them. If you have, and as a result the trust is there, great. But if you haven't had these conversations with all the members of your team, or you are new to the team and you haven't had these conversations with any of them, now is the time to make them happen. Some of the opportunities you have are:

- Informal opportunities like coffee breaks and lunch
- Walking down the corridor to another meeting
- Waiting for meetings to begin
- Attending meetings or conferences together
- Travelling – by car, taxi, train or plane
- At the very end of the day when most people have gone home
- Social events
- Team building events

Although each trust building conversation should be quite informal, you can be quite structured about making sure they happen. It can be useful to ask yourself:

1. Who would I like to have a more trusting relationship with?
2. What level of conversation would help that – factual stuff, preferences and values, feedback to you or showing vulnerability?
3. What opportunities are there to have this conversation?
4. What will I do?

FAQ about trust building conversations

1. **Some people don't like talking about personal things at work.**
   While most people appreciate being asked about things outside work, a few people prefer to keep their working lives very separate from their personal lives. So if you begin a trust building conversation by asking them the factual stuff, and they seem unwilling to discuss it, don't force it. Simply move on to the preferences and values conversation and ask them what they do and don't like about their current job. If even that seems too intrusive

for some people (Why do you want to know?), simply ask them how they are today. In some organisations levels of trust are so low that you have to begin to build trust in quite a gentle way.

2. **You can't force trust – it's either there or it isn't.**
Have you ever had a working relationship with someone whom at first you didn't much warm to, but over time, as you got to know them better, you began to like and respect? Have you ever had a working relationship with someone whom you trusted, but then things went wrong? Trust is a variable quantity, not a fixed one. The more we get to know each other, the more I seem to you to be competent, open, reliable and on your side, the more you will trust me. As soon as I do something that is incompetent, deceitful or that demonstrates that you can't rely on me, that trust will diminish or disappear.

3. **Is it easier to build trust or to lose it?**
Much easier to lose it. Building trust is slow and hard. Losing trust is quick and easy.

4. **There are some people I will never trust – so why should they trust me?**
Three useful questions to ask yourself if you don't trust someone:

i. *Are you being fair to them?*

Do you have the evidence that they are untrustworthy? Let's say someone is often late for work. Do you take that as evidence that they are unreliable, and therefore untrustworthy? If you knew that they were sometimes late for work because they had to care for an elderly parent, and that they always made up the extra time over their lunch break, would that change your view?

When people let us down, we often assume that this is due to personal qualities rather than external circumstances. So if you don't trust someone, make sure you really know what's going on. Finding out may require a different kind of courageous conversation.

ii. *Are they a member of your team?*

If you really do have evidence that they are untrustworthy, and they are a member of your team, it's your job as manager to do something about it. You will need to give them feedback about the specific things they are doing that lead you to believe that they are being untrustworthy.

iii. *Are they a colleague or a more senior manager?*

If the person is a colleague or more senior to you, you need to make a judgement call. Would that person be open to receiving feedback from you about their behaviour? If yes, then have that courageous conversation. If no, then you have to tolerate their behaviour and do the best you can. If their behaviour becomes intolerable for you, then find a job somewhere else.

Active listening

In the first two chapters of this book – about feedback and objective setting – the emphasis has been on what you say to the other person. Although both giving feedback and setting objectives should be a two-way conversation, not a monologue, we've focused on what you say to them and how.

When it comes to trust building, the emphasis changes. The questions you ask are important, but what really matters is how you listen to their replies.

You need to be listening at two levels: for the facts and for the feelings. Both are important, whatever kind of trust building conversation you are having.

Let's say you are building trust with someone you don't know very well by asking about their family. They reply, 'I've got two teenage sons, but we've also got my elderly mum living with us at the moment.' As well as taking in the factual information you also need to notice that the person seems quite upbeat when they talk about their sons, but more subdued when they talk about their mother. It's not that you should read too much into this – your assumptions about the situation might be wrong – but it's useful to notice the feelings as well as the facts.

You also need to demonstrate that you are listening. Show your interest with an appropriate amount of eye contact, a bit of nodding, and by saying 'yes' every so often. It can also help to summarise what the person has said now and again, especially if what the person says is complicated or unclear.

As well as summarising the facts the person has said, you can also attempt to summarise the feelings. It's often best to do this slightly tentatively, because you may get it wrong.

Getting the balance right

In any courageous conversation you need to get the right balance of talking and listening. If one person is doing all the talking it's not a conversation. But the balance depends very much on what kind of conversation it is. A straightforward piece of feedback can be more you talking than them. But if the initial feedback leads into more of a problem solving discussion, then the balance of talking and listening will be more equal. When you are setting objectives, the balance depends very much on how experienced the person is. If you are setting objectives for a very inexperienced person, then you may be doing most of the talking. On the other hand, if they are very experienced you may find yourself asking them a few questions using OPERA and letting them do most of the talking.

Voice and body

In a famous piece of research from the 1960s, often quoted on management training courses, Albert Mehrabian concluded that only 7% of communication depends on the words you speak. 38% depends on the tone of voice in which they are spoken and 55% depends on facial expression. This is of course nonsense. If it were true you'd never have to learn a foreign language, because you could communicate 93% of your message just by using the right tone of voice and the right facial gestures.

What Mehrabian's research actually said was that the **feelings** people get as a result of your communication depends 7% on the words, 38% on the tone and 55% on the facial expression. This does make sense. If someone says to you, 'I've got some news for you', the feelings you experience depend a great deal more on the tone of voice and facial expression than on the words themselves.

So although Mehrabian's research is often misquoted, it does draw attention to the fact that when it comes to feelings, voice tone, facial expression and also body posture and gesture make a big difference. And when people are deciding how much to trust you they will do it on the basis of feelings, not on the basis of a logical analysis of your track record.

As well as actively listening, it can also help to adopt a similar body posture to the other person. If the person you are talking to is sitting up straight, it will help them to feel at ease if you sit up straight too. But if the other person is more relaxed in their chair, perhaps with their legs stretched out and crossed, it will help if you take a more relaxed position too. Of course you can take this too far – if you self-consciously imitate every gesture and change of posture the other person makes they will find this highly disconcerting. But as a general rule, people who are sitting or standing in similar ways will find it easier to create trust and rapport with each other than those who are not.

4. MOTIVATION

Why you need to motivate people

The world of work is changing. If you were working in one of Henry Ford's car factories in the early 1900s, or like me, starting your first job as a teacher in the 1980s, you didn't expect work to be fun and fulfilling all the time. But you probably did expect to do what your boss told you. Respect for authority was higher in the twentieth century than it is now.

But in the second decade of the twenty-first century most people aspire, if not expect, to do work that is enjoyable and fulfilling. Respect for authority though, is generally lower than it was.

What does this mean for you as a manager? It means that you can't simply tell people what to do and expect them to do it happily and to a high standard. You must become an expert at motivating people.

This is even more important if your job requires you to influence and persuade people you don't line manage directly. Even if formal authority still worked, you can't use it if you haven't got that formal authority. Being able to motivate, influence and persuade people to do things is a key management skill in the twenty-first century.

Motivation is complicated. When you ask someone to do something, their motivation will depend on three key factors: the task itself, how much they trust and respect you, and the way you ask them.

The task itself

In a busy working environment it's generally easier to motivate someone to have a ten-minute break than it is to motivate them to stay an extra hour to read some policy documents. So what makes some tasks inherently more motivational than others?

It depends on the individual. People are very different. A task that motivates one person may be a complete turn-off for another. I once had a job that involved sitting down with my team, once a year, and sorting several hundred pounds' worth of bronze and silver coins into bags of different denominations. For me, this was a dull, dirty and tedious job. But for one of my team members it was highly enjoyable. He relished working on a very routine task that gave him the chance to spend time chatting and socialising with the rest of the team.

The more you get to know your team as individuals, the more you will learn about which tasks they love, and which tasks they hate. The trust building conversations described in the last chapter can help you to do this.

Having said that people are different, human beings share some common preferences when it comes to a task being motivational. Three factors are especially important.

The first is autonomy. Most people would rather do a task in their own way, rather than being forced to use someone else's approach. People whose jobs give them a lot of autonomy not only enjoy the work more, but they also have better health and live longer.

If you want to motivate someone to do a task, give them lots of clarity about what you expect them to deliver – using a tool like OPERA – and give them lots of freedom to decide how to do it. As we discussed in chapter two, letting the other person decide how to do the task not only encourages them to take responsibility, but often leads to better results.

The second common factor in motivation is mastery. This means giving people tasks they are good at. If a job is too easy people get bored. If a job is too hard they may get stressed and frustrated. But if the complexity and challenge of the task closely matches the person's level of skill, chances are they will find it enjoyable and motivating.

The third common factor in motivation is purpose. People are generally more motivated to do something they think is worthwhile. While it's easy to see that a surgeon might find her job purposeful, a hospital porter or an office cleaner can find his work equally purposeful if he believes it is making a meaningful difference.

That's why the Effect part of both the E2C2 feedback model and the OPERA objective setting model is so important. If people understand the effects of their actions, they are much more likely to be motivated to do the right thing.

Ideally, every task you ask your team members to do has a worthwhile purpose. If not, why are you asking people to do it? But it may be that some of the tasks you ask people to do are low on autonomy, because they just have to be done in a certain way, or are low on mastery because they're not that difficult to do. How do you motivate people then?

This is where external rewards come in. If a task requires judgement and creativity, then the best way to motivate people is to explain why it's worthwhile, make sure they have the skills to do it, and then let them do it in their own way. But if a task is very routine, then you can motivate people with external rewards.

Two forms of external reward are money and praise.

If you want someone to do a routine job well, pay them by results. If there's a clear link in that person's mind between a job well done and the financial reward, they will be motivated.

If you can't give them cash, buy them a coffee or give them a bunch of flowers.

As well as financial rewards, you can motivate people to do routine tasks with praise. While a simple 'well done' is better than nothing, more detailed praise using the E2C2 feedback model from chapter one is more powerful still.

If you want to motivate someone to do a routine, low skill task, then external rewards like money and praise work well. But if you want to motivate someone to do a task that requires judgement and skill, then external rewards don't work. They make performance worse.

You've not misread that last sentence. If you try to motivate someone to do a task that requires judgment and skill, external rewards will often make performance worse, not better. In these cases it's much more productive to rely on the internal motivators of autonomy, mastery and purpose.

Trust and respect

If you are asking someone to do something, their motivation to do it will depend partly on the task itself and the associated rewards. But it will also depend on how they feel about you. To be blunt, if they trust and respect you, it will be relatively easy to motivate and influence them; if they don't, it will be almost impossible.

People will respect you if they think that you are competent at your job, and live your life with integrity. You can't force people to respect you – you have to earn it through your actions.

People will trust you if they respect you *and* they believe that you care about them. Once again, you can't force people to trust you. You have to earn that trust through your actions. But you can accelerate the process by having the trust building conversations we discussed in chapter three. People won't believe that you care about them unless you find out what they really care about. That's why it's useful to have conversations about the factual stuff and their preferences and values. Trust is enhanced when people see that you are changing your behaviour in response to things they care about, and that's why feedback and vulnerability conversations help to build trust.

Although you can accelerate the trust building process, there's a natural limit to how fast it can happen. If you wait to build trust until the moment you want the person to do something, then you've probably left it too late. The more time you spend building trust in the earlier stages of any working relationship, the easier it will be to motivate people when the time comes.

How to ask using PDA

Even if you've built a high level of trust with the person you want to influence – and especially if you haven't – the way you ask people to do things makes a big difference.

Most people's intuitive way to ask someone to do something is along the lines of, 'Do this, because it's really good.' You then go on to say why it's really good.

This is usually a fairly ineffective way to motivate someone. Most human beings are innately risk-averse. If it's a choice between sticking with the old and familiar or taking on something new, most people will stick with the old and familiar. However enthusiastically you say, 'Do this, because it's really good', you are quite likely to get the response, 'I'm OK as I am thanks.' If you really want to motivate someone, you need a more powerful technique.

The technique is called PDA and it works with anyone you want to influence, whether it's a member of your team, a colleague, your boss, a customer or a supplier. It can also work with friends and family, though that's beyond the scope of this book. Here's how it works.

Present situation

Begin with the **present** situation. Talk about the downsides of the present situation and help the person to understand the impact of those downsides. Talk about how things will get worse if nothing changes.

The reason for focusing on the negatives at this stage is to create some motivation for change. Because most human beings are risk-averse, it's easier to motivate them to avoid bad things than it is by the prospect of good things happening.

Ideally you will talk about the present situation in such a way that the person you are trying to motivate thinks, 'Yes, exactly – at last someone who really understands the challenges I am facing.' You can only do this if you have had the trust building conversations described in the previous chapter.

Desired situation

Describe, in vivid detail, just how good things could be once the end goal is achieved. Talk about the benefits of the **desired** situation.

Ideally you want to talk about the personal benefits to the person you are trying to motivate. This is sometimes referred to as the WIIFM factor – What's In It For Me? The benefits to the individual may not be obvious. For one person, getting paid lots for doing something easy may be more motivational than doing a very challenging task for nothing. For another, the exact opposite may be true. Once again, you can only know the WIIFM factor if you know the person well, and that's why the trust building conversations are so important.

Sometimes there is no personal benefit to the person you are trying to motivate. Sometimes what you are asking them to do makes their life worse. If this is the case, don't pretend otherwise. If the task really is horrible, tedious and time-consuming, be honest about that.

Instead talk about the benefits to your customers, clients, or other people your organisation exists to serve. Instead of appealing to naked self-interest, you take the high moral ground. Effectively you say, 'I know this is going to make life harder for you, but this is how it will benefit our customers.'

On rare occasions you will find yourself in the position of having to motivate someone to do something that is of no benefit to them or your customers either. Senior managers in your organisation make stupid decisions. Governments force you to do things in a certain way. Key customers, suppliers or other stakeholders take decisions that make no sense to you, but leave you with no option but to comply. In this case you can't honestly talk about the benefits because there aren't any. Instead you use the 'best of a bad job' argument. Essentially you are saying, 'We have no choice about this, so why don't we make it as positive an experience as possible.' I hope you are never in this situation, but if you work in the UK public sector, chances are you'll have to face up to this kind of challenge now and again.

Action
The final part of the PDA format is **action**. If you want to motivate people to achieve the desired state, don't ask them to do it all in one go. Remember that people are risk-averse. Ask them to do something small, one-off and easy, which will lead them in the direction of the desired situation.

That's it. Present situation and downsides, desired situation and benefits, and action – the first easy step.

Make it a conversation
What if you make your pitch using PDA, but the person is unwilling to take action? Rarely is it useful to try and argue with them. Trying to prove that you are right and they are wrong almost never works.

Let's say you want someone to stop using process X and to start using process Y instead. You use PDA to point out the downsides of process X, the benefits of process Y and the first steps in the transition.

If the person responds by saying, 'I think that's a terrible idea', don't start arguing with them to try and prove that you are right and they are wrong. Instead, ask them questions and listen carefully to their answers.

You ask, 'What are your objections to this?' and they say, 'My staff haven't got time to learn process Y.' Then it may well be that they agree in principle that the current process X doesn't work very well. In which case, build on that common ground by saying something like, 'So whatever process we use has to give the best results for our customers, without being too costly or cumbersome for us to use.' If you get agreement, then you have some common ground on which to base some creative problem solving, using some of the problem solving tools in chapter five.

On the other hand, if you ask about their objections and they say, 'I don't see that there's anything wrong with process X', then you may need to say something like, 'I used to think that process X was OK too until I looked at it in more detail. What evidence would you need to see to be persuaded that process X no longer works as we need it to?'

Continue the conversation by asking questions relevant to what the other person says.

PDA in action

Zainab is a senior manager and Helen is one of her direct reports. Although Helen delivers good results, she often complains about how busy she is, and her team often complain about how she treats them. Zainab and Helen have a good working relationship, and Zainab has already given

Helen feedback about her lack of engagement with her team, but nothing much has changed. Zainab's outcome for this conversation is to motivate Helen to engage more with her team.

Zainab: Thanks for making time for us to talk. As you know, I think you deliver good results, but I'd like you to relate to your team in a different way.

Helen: Look, we've talked about this before – I know you're unhappy with the way I treat my team sometimes, but as you've said yourself, I reach most of my targets and frankly I just haven't got time to be chatting with my team members all the time.

Z: [Resisting the temptation to say, 'It's not about chatting with them all the time, it's about a small amount of focused time delegating properly', instead she talks about the present situation and the downsides.] OK, let's just take a look at how things are right now. From my perspective, you do hit most of your targets but your score in the recent staff engagement survey was in the bottom quarter of all team results. Plus over the last year you've lost two team members, both good people. Do you agree?

H: [Says nothing]

Z: I was sorry to lose both those team members but I was particularly concerned when Martin handed in his notice, because we'd invested quite a lot of time and money in developing him. Plus HR tells me it costs more than £5000 to recruit a new person. OK, from your perspective, how do you feel about things?

H: Well, as you know, I'm pleased with what I deliver, I just have too much to do.

Z: So if you could change anything, what would that be?

H: Less work? More staff? Not that that's going to happen!

Z: OK, so in an ideal world, what we'd both want is for you to continue to deliver results, to feel a bit less pressured about doing it, and to have a more engaged team. [Desired situation and benefits]

H: [Shrugs shoulders] Sure.

Z: Let me be blunt with you, Helen. I think a more engaged team would not only be a good thing in itself – one of our corporate values is about being a great place to work – but it could also help you to feel less pressured about the workload on you. As we've discussed before, the reason some of your team members gave low engagement scores isn't because they feel overworked – on the contrary, it's because they feel they're not given enough responsibility.

H: I think I know who you're talking about and I don't give him responsibility because when I do he doesn't deliver.

Z: [Resisting the temptation to say, 'The reason he didn't deliver was because you didn't delegate the task to him properly', instead she chooses a small, easy action.] I don't dispute that. And I don't underestimate the challenge for both you and your team in changing the way that you work together, so I'd like to suggest one small thing as an experiment. I'd like you to identify one member of staff who you think is capable of doing more. Some time this week, I'd like you to sit down with that person for just five minutes and ask them if they are interested in taking on more responsibility and if so what they are interested in doing. You don't have to make any commitment to them there and then – in fact I really don't want you to at this stage – just find out what they might be interested in. Are you willing to do this?

H: Sure.

Z: OK, who will it be?

H: Who do you suggest?

Z: From where I sit both Nita and Jason strike me as people with potential, but it's your team and it has to be your choice.

H: OK, well if it's just five minutes I'll talk to both of them.

Z: Good. Let's meet again at the end of this week to talk about what they said and where you want to take it from here.

When and where to use PDA

You can use PDA in any situation where you want to motivate another person, or a group of people.

You can use it in a conversation with one other person, as in the example above.

You can use it informally in a meeting. When someone asks why you are proposing something, you can structure your reply using PDA: Here's how things are now with the downsides, here's how they could be with the benefits, here's the first practical step.

You can also use it more formally when you have to make a persuasive presentation to a group of people.

FAQ about motivation

1. **Why only ask them for a small action? Why not ask them to do it all?**
    Because they are more likely to do the small thing than the big thing. Imagine you want to motivate a friend to take more exercise. You could say, 'Next time you go to the second floor, use the stairs rather than the lift.' Or you

could say, 'From now on, go jogging for 30 minutes at least three times a week.' Which is more likely to happen? Of course it's the stairs option. It's better to get people to succeed with a small thing than to fail with a big thing.

2. **How many conversations like this do you need before people do the things you really want them to do?**
    In the example above, the real-life Zainab had four conversations with Helen to get her motivated to change. The first was pretty much as you read it above. The second was to review the conversations with Nita and Jason and agree that she would delegate one small task to each of them. The third was to review how well Helen thought Nita and Jason had completed their tasks, and the fourth was to roll out this approach to the rest of her team.

    Whether you need more or less than four conversations depends on the person and the situation. It's typical to need two or three to get a positive shift, but sometimes it takes more.

3. **How much do you tell them and how much do you ask them?**
    As with every conversation you have to make a judgment about how much you tell the other person and how much you ask them for their ideas. Telling is quick, certain and can result in low commitment; asking takes longer, is uncertain but usually results in higher levels of commitment. Zainab used a fair amount of telling in her conversation with Helen. When she tried asking Helen which team member she should have that five-minute conversation with ('OK, who will it be?'), she didn't get much of a response ('Who do you suggest?'), so she suggested a couple of names – Nita and Jason. If Helen had come up with a name of her own, Zainab would have gone with that suggestion.

4. **I haven't got time to spoon-feed people like this. Why can't people just do it anyway?**

In an ideal world everyone you work with would already be highly motivated to do the things you believe are right. You may be lucky enough to lead a team of highly motivated, skilled individuals. But in the real world, you may encounter people who are not so motivated. If you already know of a better, faster way to motivate people than the PDA approach I'm suggesting here then use it (and let me know so that I can include it in the next edition of this book). But if you don't, then give PDA a try.

5. PROBLEM SOLVING

Why you need to have problem solving conversations

Although many courageous conversations begin with feedback, objective setting, trust building or motivation, they often continue into problem solving conversations.

- You give a team member some feedback about the quality of his work. He agrees that it needs to be better, but isn't sure how – and neither are you.
- You agree with a team member that she will deliver a major project this year. She's keen to take it on, but doesn't know how to get buy-in from the various project stakeholders.
- You have a very productive trust building conversation with a new team member in which he tells you that he needs more of your time to help him with a major project. You can see that he needs this help, but you haven't got the time to do it.
- You motivate a member of your team to build a relationship with a difficult client using PDA. She completes the small, easy action you suggest and then comes back to you to ask, 'What do I do now?'

As well as having problem solving discussions that have evolved from a different kind of courageous conversation, your job probably involves solving problems across a range of issues – not just about people but also about technical problems, processes, resourcing and a whole host of other things. In this chapter you will learn an approach to problem solving that you can use for any kind of problem.

Why is problem solving a courageous conversation? You may feel that you spend a lot of time at work solving problems, and that while problem solving isn't that easy, it doesn't particularly require a lot of courage either.

There are two reasons why many organisations often find themselves facing the same problems again and again. The first is a refusal to face up to a problem and give it the attention it truly deserves. The second is the tendency to adopt a quick-fix approach to problems, rather than addressing the underlying root causes in a more systematic way. Avoiding these pitfalls, and engaging in problem solving that addresses the real problems in a realistic way often does require courage.

How to solve problems using PDA2

There are four main steps to the problem solving process:

P stands for **present situation**

D stands for **desired situation**

The first **A** stands for **analysis**

The second **A** stands for **action**

The overall format is similar to the PDA format for motivation, with the additional A of analysis.

Present situation
Problem solving begins with the current situation and its downsides. Be sure that you've got the evidence that things really are a problem. If one of your colleagues comes to you to complain that a member of her team is underperforming, don't assume you know what that means. In what sense is this person underperforming – are they failing to hit targets, are they upsetting customers, are they turning up late for important meetings? How much is this happening? Has this just started

in the last week or so, or has it been going on for months? Maybe this person is erratic – weeks of high performance are followed regularly by weeks of poor performance. Before you do anything else be sure to get an accurate picture of what's going on.

Desired situation

The next step is to talk about the desired situation. How would things be if the situation were completely resolved? What are the benefits of the desired situation?

At this point it can be tempting to jump straight to the action stage and go for the quick fix. In most situations, it's worth doing some analysis first.

Analysis

Here are three especially useful questions to ask at the analysis stage:

1. Why is this happening?
2. What's already working?
3. What assumptions are we making?

1. Why is this happening?

One way to get to the root cause of a problem is to keep asking 'why?' questions.

A member of staff consistently misses deadlines. Why is this happening? It could be because they are less skilled than some of their colleagues, or they don't have the right equipment, or they have too much work to do, or some combination of these. Or is it another reason entirely?

If you establish that the reason for missed deadlines is a lack of skill, why is this happening? Is it because they weren't given training, or they were given the wrong kind of training, or you recruited the wrong person, or because the person hasn't got the capability to develop this skill?

If you establish that they weren't given the right kind of training, why was this? You get the idea – keep asking why until you get to the root causes of the problem.

Of course it's easier and quicker to blame the person and just tell them to shape up and meet deadlines in future! But if you really want to resolve this problem permanently, then you have to understand why this is happening.

2. What's already working, at least in part?

An extremely useful, and somewhat counter-intuitive question, is to ask what's already working, at least in part.

In the case of the staff member who consistently misses deadlines, are there any deadlines that she does achieve? If you discover that she misses deadlines for submitting management accounts, but always hits the deadlines for submitting her travel expenses, then that's useful information. If she misses deadlines at the end of each month, but achieves some Monday morning deadlines, that too is useful information.

If you are trying to understand what would motivate a hard-to-motivate member of staff, ask them to tell you about the times when they have been motivated.

This is sometimes called a 'solutions-focused approach' or even 'looking for the bright spots'.

3. What assumptions are we making?

One of the reasons problems are difficult to solve is because we assume certain things are true. Just because we assume something doesn't mean it's true – but it doesn't mean that it's false either. As soon as we challenge those assumptions, we open up a huge range of creative possibilities.

There are three assumptions that are very commonly made about workplace problems.

Assumption number one – people underperform because they don't want to do a good job.

There are all sorts of reasons why people underperform at work – not knowing what is expected of them, not having the skills or knowledge to do the job, not having the time or resources to do a job properly, not understanding why something is worthwhile, not being able to change bad habits.

If you make the wrong assumption about why the person is underperforming you will struggle to improve their performance. So don't assume – ask the questions that will help you to find out.

Assumption number two – I can't do more because I don't have enough time (or other key resources).

This is almost the flipside of assumption number one. Useful questions in this situation are:

- What could you do less of? What are the things that take up your time or your team's time that don't really contribute to what you are trying to achieve here?

- What new working practices could you and your team adopt that would enable you to achieve more with less?

- What new skills could you develop that would enable you to achieve more with less?

Once again, assuming that the problem is simply a lack of resources will prevent you from finding more creative solutions.

Assumption number three: we have to sit down and find the solution that will solve this problem once and for all.

Think of a reasonably challenging problem that you are facing in your team, department or organisation. Let's say that you could employ the best brains on the planet, and give them all the resources they need to come up with the best solution to that problem, *but without actually testing it out first*. How confident would you be that their solution would actually work in practice?

When I ask senior managers this question, the response I usually get is 'not very'. In fact large organisations very often do employ, if not the best brains on the planet, some very expensive management consultants to come up with answers to their problems, and frankly, their record is poor. This isn't because management consultants are stupid or senior managers are gullible. It's because of something much more fundamental about the nature of change in complex systems, and it's this: in a complex system, however much analysis you do, you can never predict with complete certainty the outcome of any solution to any problem.

If you want to solve problems in your team, department or organisation, make sure you do a certain amount of analysis to make sure you at least get to the root causes of the problem. But don't spend too much time trying to find the perfect solution. Instead, take whatever next step seems most likely to lead you in the right direction and make sure you learn from the experience of implementing it. This is another situation in which seeking and learning from feedback is critical.

Action
What's the next step? What action is most likely to lead in the direction of the desired situation? What can you do to make sure that you seek and receive feedback about the impact of

that action in order to inform the next stage of the problem solving process?

Effective problem solving – like effective feedback, objective setting, trust building and motivation – is a series of courageous conversations, not just a one off. That's why this management stuff is so hard, and ultimately so rewarding.

Problem solving in action

Here's how Zainab uses the PDA2 problem solving approach with Helen in her next meeting.

Zainab: How did you get on with Nita and Jason?

Helen: Fine.

Z: What did they say when you asked them about taking on more responsibility?

H: Well, as I could have predicted, they both said they'd like to have bigger and more challenging projects to do when their current projects finish. The problem is though that when I've given them bigger pieces of work in the past they've messed up and I've ended up doing it myself.

Z: OK, so the present situation is that you feel overworked and under-resourced. You can't trust Nita and Jason to take on bigger projects.

H: Correct.

Z: But in an ideal world you would be able to trust Nita and Jason with bigger projects so that they could take some of the pressure off of you?

H: Of course.

Z: OK, I want to analyse why this is happening. Why do you think Nita and Jason have messed up in the past with bigger projects?

H: Mmm, I'd say with Nita, she doesn't always think things through before making a decision, and with Jason it's almost the opposite – he lacks confidence to take action even though he probably knows what to do.

Z: That rings true to me. And if I'm honest, when you delegated the last round of projects to Nita and Jason, you gave them a written brief but didn't spend much time talking it through with them, did you?

H: That's a bit harsh, but yeah, I didn't have the time to spend with them.

Z: So to put it another way, you assumed that once they had the written brief they should be left to get on with it?

H: Yes, I did.

Z: Let's challenge that assumption. I think that this time round, if you spend more time with them talking through the project brief, then they're more likely to do a better job.

H: I can't disagree with that, it just seems that it's going to take up even more of my time…

Z: Well, maybe a bit more in the short term, yes. OK, let me suggest some alternative ways forward here. You can give either Nita or Jason or both a bigger project to do. You can sit down to talk them through the project brief – I've got a really nifty model called OPERA that will help you to do that. And you could also – who's best at projects in your team?

H: Siobhan.

Z: You could also get Nita or Jason to sit down with Siobhan to run through the brief or even get some mentoring from her during their next big project. So lots of alternative courses of action there – what do you think?

H: Well, I'd like both Nita and Jason to take on a bigger project and I'll commit to explaining the brief to them. Email me the OPERA stuff and I'll take a look at it. I think Nita and Siobhan would work well together but maybe Jason needs someone else to help him with his confidence.

Z: Like who?

H: If I'm honest it probably needs to be me. I've been a bit short with him in the past.

Z: That sounds like a plan. So just sum up for me in your words exactly what you are going to do and when…

Here are some things to notice about that conversation.

Zainab followed the structure – present state with downsides, desired state with benefits, analysis and action.

It was a conversation: although Zainab was structuring and controlling the overall conversation, sometimes Helen was making the suggestions and sometimes Zainab was.

Zainab made a judgment about how much analysis to do.

When and where to do problem solving with PDA2

You can use the PDA approach to problem solving whenever you encounter a problem that needs solving. You can use it on your own to structure your thinking, you can use it with one other person in a problem solving conversation, and you can use it to structure a problem solving session with a larger group.

As well as general problem solving opportunities there are two specific situations when you might want to use PDA2 as part of a courageous conversation.

The first of these situations is when you have already had a courageous conversation to agree **what** needs to happen, but you are not quite sure **how** to make it happen. You may have given someone some feedback about the way they interact with customers, and reached agreement that they need to handle customers differently. But how exactly? This is where problem solving conversations can help.

You may have used OPERA to define the outcomes of a major project with one of your team members. The team member then asks you for advice on dealing with some of the project stakeholders. As well as sharing your experience, doing some problem solving can also be very effective. You may have motivated someone to take on a new area of responsibility and they need ideas on how to fulfil their new role. Once again a problem solving approach can help.

The second situation where problem solving can be extremely useful is where there is conflict.

Sometimes at work you will find yourself in conflict with someone else, and sometimes you may find yourself having to resolve conflicts between others.

Typically conflict goes something like this. Person A wants one thing, and person B wants another. They argue. Person A usually ignores B's wishes and focuses on why they must have whatever they want. Person B usually ignores A's wishes and focuses on why they must have whatever they want. Sometimes the tone is relatively polite and there is some bargaining: A might be willing to give way on something small providing B gives something in return. We call this negotiation. Sometimes the tone is not at all polite and there are threats and insults. We call this organisational politics.

The key to resolving conflict of any kind is to find some common ground, and then switch to problem solving mode. If you find yourself in conflict with a colleague, ask yourself, what do we both want? If you both work for the same organisation there is a good chance that you both want your customers to be happy, even if you have differing views about how that is to be achieved. Once you've established common ground, problem solving becomes a possibility.

FAQ about problem solving

1. **What's the difference between motivation using PDA and problem solving using PDA2?**
    If you are completely sure what needs to happen then motivate the other person (or people) using PDA. But if you are not sure what needs to happen – you just know that things are not so good at the moment – then you need to problem solve using PDA2.

    Having said that, you may find yourself moving from 'motivation mode' into 'problem solving mode' during the course of a single conversation. Having motivated someone to produce better quality reports, for example, you might then switch to problem solving mode to discuss how this person can acquire the skills of being able to write a high quality report.

    Quite often you will use a feedback, objective setting or motivation conversation to agree the 'what' and the 'why', and then move to a problem solving conversation to agree the 'how'.

2. **Who should you involve in a problem solving conversation?**

   This depends on the nature of the problem. Sometimes it might be just one other person, and sometimes you might involve a group of people who have something to contribute. Usually this will be less than about half a dozen people. If you have more then you will need to structure and facilitate the meeting very carefully.

   Whether one or more others are involved, make sure that everyone contributes ideas. If you are making people listen while you think out loud, this isn't really problem solving, and if you rely on the other person to come up with all the ideas this is more coaching than problem solving. Good problem solving is usually characterised by the fact that everyone contributes ideas to the process.

3. **Who takes action?**

   When you are discussing a problem with one or more of your team members or colleagues, who should take the action? Whoever is best placed to do so. Make sure your language reflects this. If you want the other person to take action, say, 'What are you going to do?' not, 'What are we going to do?' If you are going to take action, say, 'This is what I'm going to do', not, 'This is what we're going to do.' Reserve the use of 'we' for when you genuinely need it, as in, 'We will meet again next Tuesday.'

4. **Can this PDA2 approach work for solving any kind of problem?**

   The overall format works well for solving most kinds of problems. When you are working on more technical problems, to do with processes, procedures, equipment or design, you may want to use more specialist tools to help you, particularly at the analysis phase of the process. You may also want to be more systematic in how you identify and test what you will do in the action phase, but the overall approach is pretty similar.

The one situation where you may want to skip straight from the present situation to action, without much in the way of analysis (and in some cases without even the desired situation either) is if you take an intuitive approach to problem solving.

Do you ever encounter a problem at work and you just have a hunch or a gut feeling about what you need to do to tackle that problem? If you have a lot of experience of dealing with this kind of problem, then it's often worth following your intuition and using that as the basis for action – providing you are willing to seek and respond to the resulting feedback.

Intuitive problem solving has the advantage that it's very much faster than doing the sort of thorough analysis I'm suggesting here. But if you don't have much experience, or your experience is out of date, then the danger of intuitive problem solving is that it can come up with precisely the wrong solution. Intuition, gut feeling and instinct are powerful forces: be sure to use them appropriately.

5. **Is creativity important for problem solving?**
    My favourite definition of creativity in business is this: think about what your customer would like but that currently seems impossible – and then find a way to provide it.

    We tend to think of creativity in terms of products – the smartphone or the tablet computer – but it applies equally to new processes or new solutions to old problems. The key to creativity is to challenge assumptions. When Steve Jobs at Apple invented the smartphone, he challenged the assumption that mobile phones, portable music players and devices for accessing the Internet were all separate. When Herb Kelleher at Southwest Airlines invented the low cost airline, he did it by challenging the assumption that air travel had to be luxurious.

When Patty McCord at Netflix decided to scrap formal performance appraisal, she did it by challenging the assumption that an organisation's formal performance appraisal actually improves performance.

Creativity is an important part of problem solving, but you don't need to worry about whether or not you think you are creative – you just need to start challenging the assumptions that everyone else is making.

6. COACHING

Why you need to coach people

A coaching conversation is similar to a problem solving conversation in many ways. You begin with the present situation and the downsides; you discuss the desired situation and the benefits; you analyse the situation to help you come up with some creative ways forward; and you take some action.

The difference is this: with problem solving both of you are contributing ideas to solving the problem. With coaching it's only the person being coached who contributes ideas. Your job is to ask helpful questions and keep the discussion on track.

Why would you want to do that? Whatever you are coaching the other person about, chances are you have some ideas or opinions yourself – why hold back? There are three reasons. Firstly, the other person is more likely to take action if they come up with the ideas rather than you. Secondly, your ideas and opinions might not actually be that helpful. Thirdly, the person is likely to learn more if they reflect on their own ideas than if you simply tell them what to do.

The other way in which coaching is different from problem solving is the emphasis on generating and evaluating alternative courses of action. Problem solving is PDA2 – present situation, desired situation, analysis, action. Coaching is PDA3 – present situation, desired situation, analysis, *alternatives* and action.

Examining alternatives not only increases the chances that the final course of action is going to be the right one, but it also enhances the learning for the person being coached.

The outcome of an effective coaching session isn't just that the person commits to a good course of action, it's also that they've learnt from the process. Some coaching conversations aren't really about problem solving at all – they are about helping people to learn from their experiences.

How to structure a coaching session with PDA3

When you are coaching your main job is to ask the right questions and keep the person on track. Here are some useful questions you can ask under each heading.

Present situation and downsides
Some useful questions to get people started are:

- What do you want to talk about?
- What's the problem you are having?
- What's bothering you?

Usually the downsides of the current situation are pretty clear from what the person is saying, but sometimes it's useful to ask:

- How do you feel about this?
- Why is this a problem?
- What are the downsides of this situation?

Show the person that you are listening to what they say by giving them an appropriate amount of eye contact, nodding occasionally, and summarising what they say. Above all be empathetic – demonstrate that you understand the situation and the other person's feelings.

Resist the temptation to give your opinion on the situation – just do lots of active listening.

Don't spend too long on this stage of the conversation. Spend long enough for the other person to feel that you are taking them seriously, but not so long that you are just wallowing in how awful it is.

In some work situations, just listening to the person is all you need to do. Sometimes the most effective thing you can do is to listen respectfully and allow them to go away and tackle the situation in their own way. But often the person can do with some more help. Do this by moving on to the desired situation and benefits.

Desired situation and benefits
Useful questions at this stage are:

- What is it you want?
- What would this situation be like if it was completely resolved?
- If you could wave a magic wand to make things better, how would it be?
- How would you know things had improved?
- What would you see, hear and feel if this situation were sorted?

Usually the benefits of the desired situation are obvious, but sometimes it's useful to ask:

- How would you feel if things were sorted?
- How would this make things better?
- What are the benefits of what you're suggesting?

The key thing at this stage is to help the person gain some clarity about what the desired state would be. Quite often people stop themselves from thinking about the desired state because they believe it's unachievable. That may be so, but from a coaching point of view it's still important to talk about the ideal desired situation so that you are not unnecessarily eliminating any options at this stage.

You may or may not agree with the person's desired situation. When you are coaching it's your job to help the person identify their desired situation, not to impose yours. So if your desired situation is radically different to theirs, don't tell them. Think what questions you could ask them to expand and challenge their view of the desired situation.

Analysis

Once you've helped the person to gain a clear view of their desired situation you need to spend a bit of time analysing what's going on. Some useful questions are:

1. Why is this happening?
2. What's already working?
3. What assumptions are you making?

These questions will be familiar from chapter five on problem solving.

This analysis stage deserves a bit of time and can sometimes feel a bit messy. But it's possibly the most important part of the whole process. If the person already knew what to do to get from the present situation to the desired situation there's a good chance that they already would have done it. They're asking for your help because they're stuck. This analysis stage helps the person to see new perspectives on the situation so they know what to do next.

Alternatives

Here are some questions to help the person generate some alternative courses of action:

1. What could you do about this?
2. What could you do that you haven't yet tried?
3. Apart from the obvious solution, what else could you do?
4. Who do you admire? What would they do in this situation?
5. What would you do if it didn't feel so risky?
6. If you had unlimited resources what would you do about this?

You're unlikely to use all of these questions in a single coaching session. Choose the ones that will most help the person to generate some alternative courses of action. Ideally you should aim to help the person generate at least three alternative courses of action, although some situations may require more.

Here are some useful questions you can ask to help the person evaluate the different options they have generated.

1. What are the pros and cons of each of the options?

2. On a 0 to 10 scale, where 0 is low and 10 is high, how do you feel about these different alternatives?

3. Please evaluate these options on a 0 to 10 scale in terms of how effectively they'll deal with your problem, where 0 is not at all, and 10 is it'll be completely resolved forever. Then evaluate them on a 0 to 10 scale in terms of how easy it will be to do, where 0 is impossible to do and 10 is very easy indeed.

As you can guess, I'm quite keen on 0 to 10 scales. When a person is finding it hard to rationally evaluate their alternatives, it can be helpful to ask them to choose a number quite quickly, without thinking about it too much.

It can sometimes be useful to observe how people are talking about the various alternatives they have generated. When you ask people to sum up the options, do they talk about all the options in the same tone of voice and with equal enthusiasm? Or does their tone of voice and body language at least hint that they prefer one option ahead of another?

Action
Once the person has chosen their preferred alternative, you may feel that the coaching session is over. It isn't – not until

the person has committed to taking some very specific action. Useful questions are:

1. What are you going to do?
2. When will you do it by?
3. What resources will you need?
4. Who else needs to be involved?

Finally, it may be useful to agree to a follow-up session with the person when they tell you what they have done.

In the previous chapter on problem solving we discussed how problems are rarely resolved all in one go; what matters is to agree the action that is most likely to lead in the direction of the desired situation. This is even more true of coaching. The key thing is to get the person to take some action.

Coaching in action

Pam, a classroom teacher, asks her head teacher Sarah for advice about giving feedback to a new teacher in the school.

Pam: Have you got a minute? I need some advice.

Sarah: Sure.

P: As you know I've been observing our newly qualified teacher. I watched him doing a music lesson. He sat the children down, had them listen to quite a long piece of music and asked them to identify all the different instruments. Most of the children looked bored and the whole thing didn't go very well.

S: So, what's the thing you wanted advice on?

P: Well, he's asked me for feedback, which is fine, but although he's very enthusiastic about the music, to be honest this activity did not go well, and I want to know how I can manoeuvre him into thinking about it differently.

S: So you've observed the lesson and you want to give him feedback so that he can do better... but without denting his confidence. Is that right?

P: Yes, sort of. I would normally beat around the bush a bit with this sort of thing, but I'm not sure that's the best way to go.

S: OK, so a good outcome from this conversation we're having now would be a clear plan for giving him some feedback that gets him to deliver more engaging lessons but doesn't dent his confidence.

P: That's it.

S: So tell me a bit more about what you observed in the lesson. What worked well, and what do you think could have been better?

P: The actual activity – listen to a piece of music and spot the instruments – was fine. The piece was too long though, and the music was too complicated, and he didn't really prep them for the exercise. If it had been me, I would have given the children a list of instruments and asked them to tick each one as they heard it.

S: And why do you think he didn't do this – was it that he just didn't have the experience to know the best way to do it, or was he unwilling to put in the preparation time, or... what was going on here do you think?

P: He's certainly not unwilling to do the prep. Some of the other feedback I've given him is about over-preparing and not being flexible enough when he sees how the children respond. No, I think it's mainly lack of experience, maybe coupled with being too much of a musician and not enough of a teacher, if that makes sense.

84

S: OK, so the issue here is primarily lack of experience...
[Pam nods] How would you normally approach this?

P: Normally I'd spend quite a lot of time telling him how
difficult it is to be a new teacher, and how hard he's working,
and maybe ask him how he thought the lesson went?

S: OK, that's one approach. What else could you do?

P: I could just go straight in and ask him about how he thought
the lesson went?

S: Both of those approaches could work, but what if he thinks
the lesson went just fine?

P: Well, then I could just tell him what I think, just as I've told
you.

S: That's another option... Of all the teachers you've
encountered in your career, who do you admire most?

P: It's probably my very first head – Edith Bush she was called!

S: And how would she have handled this situation?

P: She'd have been very direct. She'd have just told him what
she thought and how he should do it next time. For her it was
all about the kids – whatever you did had to be the best for the
children.

S: OK, so given these different alternative courses of action,
what are you going to do?

P: Well, I know what I ought to do, and that's to be quite direct
about what he did and how he should do it next time.

S: Is that what you're going to do?

P: Yes… it's just that I don't want to knock his confidence.

S: So how can you give a clear message about what he needs to change and at the same time increase his confidence?

P: Well, I need to let him know that overall he's doing quite well, and that he has the potential to be a really good teacher, if he tweaks things a bit. The activities he's doing are basically pretty good, but the way he does them could be improved. I might even tell him about Miss Bush and how I got some pretty tough feedback from her when I was a new teacher. Although it wasn't always easy to hear, I wanted to be as good a teacher as I possibly could and I knew that her feedback, advice, whatever you call it, was only intended to help.

S: Sounds good to me – so when are you going to meet him and have this conversation?

P: We've already arranged to meet after school today. Thanks for that, Sarah, your advice has really helped!

Here are some things to notice about Sarah's coaching session with Pam.

Sarah did follow the PDA3 format. Pam began with the present situation (she observed the newly qualified teacher and the children looking bored) and Sarah summarised the desired situation (a clear plan for giving him some feedback that gets him to deliver more engaging lessons but doesn't dent his confidence). She spent a bit of time on analysis (what did he do well? What could have been better? Why do you think he was doing this?) and she helped Pam to generate some alternatives (how would you normally do this? What else could you do? Who do you admire and what would they do?). Finally she made sure that Pam committed to action.

Having said all that, the conversation did not feel like a very formal coaching session – it was more like a helpful chat.

Although there's nothing wrong with taking quite a formal approach to coaching in some circumstances, it's often more appropriate to take a more informal approach, as in this example.

At no point did Sarah offer advice, or tell Pam what to do. There's nothing wrong with giving advice, and in many situations it's the right thing to do. In this case, though, Sarah judged that a coaching approach would be better, for the reasons I outlined at the start of this chapter – it leads to more commitment, better outcomes and more learning for the person being coached.

The thing you can't see from this record of their conversation is their body language and tone of voice. Throughout the conversation, Sarah indicated that she was listening and interested in what Pam was saying with eye contact, nodding occasionally and adopting a similar posture to Pam. There's a section on active listening in chapter three on trust building conversations.

When and where to use coaching

Have you ever been in a situation where a member of your team comes to complain about something? They have too much work to do, or they have to deal with a difficult person, or they have a tough technical problem to crack. You find yourself giving advice, saying, 'Have you thought about...' But each piece of advice you offer is turned down. The other person may even use the phrase, 'Yes, but...' as in, 'Yes, but I can't do that because...' or, 'Yes I've tried that and it didn't work.' In these situations continuing to give advice probably won't work. This may be because your advice genuinely isn't helpful or it may be because most human beings generally prefer doing what they think is right rather than what someone else tells them to do.

Sometimes when someone comes to moan like this, all they want to do is moan. They are not really interested in doing anything about it, at least not now, and they just want some kind of recognition that life is tough. If you sense that this is what they want, listen carefully while they have their say, and then move on.

But sometimes when someone comes to moan to you, they really do want some ideas – just not yours! So when they complain about how bad things are now, instead of offering solutions, ask them how they would like things to be. Then move on to analysis, alternatives and action, remembering only to ask questions and listen. Remember that the person is far more likely to act on their own ideas than if you simply tell them what to do.

Another situation where you might consider coaching is where your expertise is lacking. Imagine one of your team members asks you for some suggestions on how to resolve a problem with one of your company's suppliers.

If you've dealt with this supplier before, and have a lot of experience of negotiating with suppliers, you're probably going to choose to have this conversation in problem solving mode – you'll put in your ideas and the other person will put in theirs.

But if you've never dealt with this particular supplier, and your experience of dealing with suppliers is quite out of date, then you'll probably choose to have this conversation in coaching mode. Although you might be quite tempted to give advice, the danger is that this advice might be irrelevant, out of date or plain wrong. Better to coach the person.

Finally, and most significantly, you can use coaching when you want the other person to learn. If someone encounters a problem, and you tell them what to do, they will know how to deal with that specific problem (assuming your solution works). But if you coach them, and help them to analyse the problem, and come up with a range of alternative solutions, then not only have they probably gained an insight into a range of related problems, but they have also effectively learnt how to solve problems for themselves.

Sometimes you can lead an effective coaching session using only some of the PDA3 stages. Someone comes to you and asks, 'Should I do X or should I do Y?' Instead of giving your opinion, ask them to weigh up the alternatives, perhaps using questions like 'What are the pros and cons of each?' or 'What's your gut feeling about what you should do?' Listen a bit and then invite them to commit to action. You've coached them just by asking questions about alternatives and action. Simply asking the person one or two questions may not feel like coaching, but it is. Whenever you refrain from giving advice, and instead ask useful questions to help the other person decide, you are coaching.

FAQ about coaching

1. **How long does a coaching session last?**

   It depends on the person and the situation. In the example above, Sarah and Pam spent about ten minutes on the real life conversation. Most coaching sessions tend to take longer, though some may be shorter.

   You don't have to work through all five elements of PDA3 all in one go. With a complex piece of coaching you may choose to separate out some of the elements into different coaching sessions.

2. **How much time should you spend on the different elements of PDA3?**

   This also depends on the person and the situation. As a rule of thumb, try not to spend too much time on the present situation. It's easy to find yourself being overly sympathetic to the person's current challenges, and to wallow in the misery a bit. As soon as the person is clear on the present situation and the downsides, move them on to desired situation and benefits.

The more experienced you become with coaching, the more you will develop an intuitive sense of when it is time to move on to the next stage of the process. This is particularly true of the analysis stage; keep asking questions until you have a sense that you have got to the heart of the problem.

In the alternatives part of the coaching session, it's often useful to generate three alternatives before asking the person to evaluate them and commit to a course of action.

This is the most important part of the coaching session – getting the person to take action. As we discussed in the problem solving chapter, you don't have to resolve the whole situation, just identify the action that's most likely to lead to the desired situation.

Although the PDA3 steps have a logical flow to them, you don't necessarily have to stick to this order. You may find it useful to jump back and forth between steps. For example, the discussions at the analysis stage may suggest that it's useful to revisit the desired situation.

3. **What about the GROW model?**
    If you've done coaching at work before, you may have come across the GROW model. It's a way to structure a coaching session, with GROW usually being defined as Goals, Reality, Options and Way forward. It's very similar to PDA3:

    Present situation – Reality
    Desired situation – Goals
    Analysis
    Alternatives – Options
    Action – Way forward

In PDA3, the first step is to talk about the present situation, but in GROW the first step is to talk about goals. Personally, I think it's more natural to talk about how things are now before talking about how you would like them to be, and that's why I prefer PDA3. Also, the GROW acronym doesn't put as much emphasis on the analysis stage, which for me is key in helping the person to get new perspectives on their problem. Having said that, 'GROW' is certainly a catchier acronym than 'PDA3'.

Common coaching problems

Great coaching is more of an art than a science. If you want to be a great coach, you'll have to practise a lot and learn from your experience. As you practise, you'll probably encounter some problems along the way. Here are some common problems you may encounter when coaching, and some questions you can ask to help move the conversation forward:

Person is too vague or too complicated:

1. Give me a specific example of when this happened.
2. Tell me the story.
3. What's the key issue for you here?

Person gives too much detail:

1. Please summarise that in 10 seconds.
2. What's the single most important thing about this situation?
3. What's the common theme here?
4. What's the general principle behind all this?

Person doesn't know what they want:

1. If you could change just one thing about this, however small, to make it a bit better, what would you say?
2. I know you don't know what you want, but if you did, what would you say?

3. What thoughts are running through your head right now?
4. If you don't know, what could you do to find out?

Person doesn't believe change is possible:

1. Has anyone ever encountered a similar situation to this? What did they do?
2. How possible do you think it is to change this on a 0 to 10 scale, where 0 is impossible to change and 10 is very easy to change?
3. What would need to happen for you to believe that change is possible here?

You think the desired situation is undesirable or unrealistic:

1. What are the pros and cons of that outcome?
2. How desirable do you think this is on a 0 to 10 scale?
3. How realistic do you think this is on a 0 to 10 scale?
4. What's your evidence for believing this?

Person has very fixed views:

1. What's potentially good about this situation?
2. What assumptions are you making about this situation?
3. If our roles were reversed, what advice would you give me about this situation?

Lack of self-awareness/blaming others for the situation:

1. Where does this happen?
2. What's your usual behaviour?
3. What skills are you using?
4. What does this say about you as a person/what are your values in this situation?
5. How would person X describe this problem?
6. How do you think person X feels about what you are doing?
7. How would an impartial observer describe this situation?

Person can't generate enough possible solutions to the problem:

1. When have you been successful in the past with a similar situation? What did you do?
2. What's good about this situation? How could you build on that?
3. What assumptions are you making here? What if you challenged those assumptions?
4. Who do you admire? How would they deal with this problem?
5. If you had unlimited resources how would you resolve this problem?
6. If you *had* to solve this problem what would you do?
7. What could you do to make the situation worse?
8. What's the one change in this situation that would change everything?
9. What further information or resources do you need to help you deal with this problem?

Possible solutions seem undesirable or unrealistic:

1. Let's just explore this for a few moments... how could that work out in practice?
2. What's your reservation about this? How could that objection be overcome?
3. What resources would you need to be able to do this?
4. Paint me a picture/tell me the story/give me a feel of how that would work out in practice.

Person can't choose between different alternatives:

1. What are the pros and cons of those different options?
2. Let's evaluate those options in terms of how effective they would be, and how easy they would be to implement.
3. You don't have to choose any of these right now, but if you did, which one would you choose? Why?
4. What's your gut feeling?
5. If you were advising someone else, what would you tell them to do?

Person won't commit to action:

1. If you do nothing, what will happen to this situation – will it become worse or better?
2. What's a small practical action that you can commit to?
3. Being realistic about how busy you are, by when will you have taken action on this?

Person commits but you don't believe them:

1. What might prevent you from taking action? What could you do about that?
2. On a scale of 0 to 10 how committed are you to taking this action? What would need to happen to increase your score?
3. Will you send me an email telling me what you are going to do? By when?
4. Do you want to meet me again to review progress? When?

7. CREATING NEW HABITS

Why habits matter

Some years ago I was caught on a speed camera doing 37mph in a 30mph zone. Given the choice of paying a fine or attending a speed awareness course, I chose the course. It was an excellent experience. As well as being an informative and engaging course, it changed my attitude towards speeding. In the past I'd interpreted speed limits somewhat flexibly, but I left the course determined to observe all speed limits from then on.

And so I did for few weeks.

Then both my daughters went away for a month, one to India and one on a trip round Europe. It so happened that they were both returning on the same day, at almost the same time, but to different airports – one to Manchester and one to Leeds/Bradford. My wife and I collected our youngest daughter from Manchester and I then drove briskly towards Leeds/Bradford Airport. I didn't notice the 30mph limit as we were driving through Halifax until the speed camera flashed, curiously enough capturing me once again at 37mph. This time I had to pay the fine.

What went wrong? I really was determined to keep to the speed limit after the course, but somehow on that particular day I just forgot. Knowing that you want to do something and having the skills to do something isn't enough to do it consistently. You also have to make it a new habit. I wanted to drive safely within the limit, and I certainly had the skills to do so. I just hadn't made it a habit.

I hope that if you've made it here to the last chapter of this book, you want to have more courageous conversations. I hope that the models, examples and explanations in this book will help you to develop the skills you need to have more courageous conversations. But you will only have more courageous conversations if you make them a habit.

Creating new habits

Here's how the people featured in this book developed new habits of courageous conversations.

Dawn – giving feedback with E2C2

To be honest, I never gave much feedback in the past – I'd avoid it if I could and hope that things would get better anyway. But on the rare occasions where I did give feedback, I'd say things like, 'Why did you do that?' or 'Didn't you think?' I was never very comfortable with this approach because I like to think I'm an honest and straightforward person, but I obviously wasn't coming across like that when I was giving feedback.

I really like E2C2. The first few times I used it I had to almost force myself to use it. I had a couple of tricky situations to deal with. I prepared quite carefully and wrote down what I needed to say for evidence, effect, continue and change. Those first conversations went surprisingly well, and that gave me the confidence to use it more. Now whenever I notice someone in my team doing something that needs my attention I automatically think in terms of E2C2. It's become a bit of a habit.

Liam – receiving feedback

In the past, as soon as I got any critical feedback I would go into defensive mode – interrupt the person to justify why I'd done whatever it was. Funnily enough I even got quite defensive when people gave me positive feedback! Instead of listening I'd interrupt and say things like 'It was nothing' or 'You'd have done the same'.

To begin with, I had to work quite hard to stop myself interrupting the person. What helped was having some good probing questions to ask instead. I think it's easier to do something different than it is to stop doing something completely. It has got a bit easier, listening to critical feedback, but to be honest, it still isn't that easy. I have to keep reminding myself that even if it feels a bit painful at the time, ultimately it's making me a better person. I have a little card on my desk that just says 'listen'. My staff like to joke about it, but it does help.

Duncan – setting objectives

I used to be a bit laid back about setting objectives. I used to think that if you just gave people an overall sense of direction and let them get on with it, then that was all a manager had to do. While I still believe that this approach works with some people, it certainly doesn't work with everyone, and I really like OPERA as a checklist of everything you have to cover. What's convinced me is the better results I've got from my team since I started using it.

When I did the training course they gave us a small laminated card with OPERA on it. I always have that to hand when I'm doing any kind of objective setting or delegation. At first I used to refer to it quite consciously, but now it just reminds me to follow the right steps when I'm setting goals.

Zainab – motivating and problem solving

In the past I've always tried to motivate people by being super-encouraging. In fact I once even did a management training course that was all about 'catching people doing things right'. I was quite comfortable with that approach apart from the obvious fact that it didn't always work.

When I first learnt about PDA I was a little uncomfortable about beginning with the downsides of the situation. But once I'd tried it a couple of times I could see that it would deliver results. I want to be thought of as a manager who gets results. So whenever I'm tempted to be overly nice, I try to remind myself that what matters is getting results – and that the opposite of nice isn't nasty, it's sometimes just being more honest.

It's not been difficult for me to adapt PDA2 as a format for problem solving. I've always felt that the company culture pushes us towards quick fixes instead of analysing the situation properly, so having the PDA2 format really helps me personally to do what I would naturally want to do anyway.

Sarah – coaching
The hardest thing for me about coaching is not jumping in with my own solutions. This might sound a little odd, but when I'm having a coaching conversation with one of my staff members I can often hear a little voice inside my head saying, 'Go on, tell her to do this.' But noticing that little voice is a help, because then I can consciously choose whether or not to give that advice. Very often these days I choose not to, because I know how powerful coaching is.

I'd say the major drawback of coaching is that it does take longer than just telling the other person what to do, at least in the short term. But I really believe that coaching helps the other person to grow and develop far more than if you just told them what to do. I really believe in the value of learning and developing – that's why I came into teaching in the first place.

Changing Habits
Here are some of the things that helped these people to change habits.

To begin with, you have to practise the habit – consciously. It might feel a little strange at first, but it's worth persevering until the new approach becomes a habit. Preparation, reminders and checklists can all be useful at this stage.

It helps to maintain the new habit if you are aware of the benefits. Dawn, Duncan and Zainab all mentioned that getting results helped them to maintain the new habit.

It also helps to maintain a new habit if you remind yourself how the new habit is consistent with your own values and beliefs. Our instinctive behaviour does not always support the things we believe in. I truly believe in the importance of eating healthily, but put me in a room with plates of unhealthy cakes and my instinctive reaction is to grab one and start eating. It's often the case that our instincts reward us in the short term (that lovely sugar rush from eating the cake now), while our values reward us in the long term (abstaining from bad food means I stay fit and healthy).

Sarah's instinct as a head teacher was to tell people what to do, the short-term reward being that she could get more done in a busy day. But her values about helping people to learn and develop helped her to develop a new habit of coaching. If you want to change a habit, it can be useful to think about your own values – what do you really believe in, and what habits would align with those beliefs?

Peer pressure and organisational culture

An often overlooked factor in creating and maintaining habits is peer pressure. If I am driving on a road where everyone else is speeding, I am much more likely to drive fast as well. In a room bursting with cream cakes of all descriptions, I am more likely to have one if everyone else is gorging too.

When someone new joins your organisation, they will be surrounded by people with a particular set of habits, and it's likely that they soon will pick up these habits. Some of these habits will be good ones. If most of the team habitually treat customers respectfully, then there's plenty of peer pressure on the new team member to treat customers respectfully too. But some of these habits might be bad ones. If most of the team habitually gossip about their boss but avoid giving him straight feedback, then the new team member will probably join in. It's not that we are completely lacking in free will, it's just that the power of peer pressure is surprisingly strong. In the context of work, this pressure to behave like everyone else is known as organisational culture.

What is the culture of your organisation when it comes to courageous conversations?

Do people give each other honest and constructive feedback; agree clear objectives; take time to build trust and motivate people to do the right things? Do they have a robust approach to problem solving and do they develop people's skill and commitment through coaching?

Or do they avoid the difficult conversations and gossip behind people's backs instead? Do they issue vague instructions and expect people to know what to do? Are they too busy to build trust and motivate people, relying on formal authority and even bullying instead? Do they go for the quick fix and just tell people what to do?

If these are two extremes of organisational culture, where is your team right now? Where would you like it to be?

Organisational culture matters. It used to be a bit of a cliché to say that people are the organisation's greatest asset. This has never been true – it's what people do at work that makes the difference. Organisations with the right culture thrive and improve the lives of all the organisational stakeholders. Organisations with the wrong culture are ineffective or worse.

Although it's tricky to change the culture across the whole of your organisation, you can change the culture in your bit of it, especially if you are in some kind of management or leadership position. The most important thing is to role model the kind of culture you want. If you want more honest feedback throughout your team, you have to start with giving – and receiving – feedback yourself. If you want more clarity of objectives, you need to make sure that you are utterly clear in the objectives you agree with others. And so on.

There are other things you can also do to change the culture: telling stories about the kind of culture you want, rewarding people who live the desired culture and aligning formal systems and procedures with the desired culture can all help. But role modelling by you – and other influential people in your team – is the first and most important step.

Having courageous conversations doesn't just benefit you and the person you're having the conversation with. By role modelling a better culture, it can have a lasting positive impact on all the people in your team – and all the people they interact with too. Courageous conversations are the key to creating high performing organisations where people love to work.

SUMMARY OF KEY MODELS

1. Feedback

Giving feedback with E2C2
E – Evidence. What did the person do?
E – Effect. What are the effects of whatever the person did?
C – Continue. What do you want them to continue doing?
C – Change. What do you want them to change?

Continuing the conversation
A – Do you **A**gree?
H – What needs to **H**appen for you to be able to do this?
A – What **A**ction will you take as a result of this?

Receiving feedback
Listen
Probe
Respond

2. Setting objectives with OPERA

O – Objective
P – Parameters – how will we measure success?
E – Effects – why is this worth doing?
R – Resources – what resources do you need?
A - Accountability

3. Building trust

Level one – basic facts
Level two – preferences and values
Level three – asking for feedback
Level four – being vulnerable

4. Motivation with PDA

P – Present situation and downsides
D – Desired situation and benefits
A – Action – simple, easy first step.

5. Problem solving with PDA2

P – Present situation and downsides
D – Desired situation and benefits
A – Analysis
A – Action – simple, easy first step.

6. Coaching with PDA3

P – Present situation and downsides
D – Desired situation and benefits
A – Analysis
A – Alternatives
A – Action – simple, easy first step.

FURTHER RESOURCES

If you want to learn more about courageous conversations at work, then visit www.ccatwork.com

You can sign up for our free leadership tips. Each week we will deliver to your inbox a practical tip on having more courageous conversations.

You can learn more about our development programmes. We help people at work to have more courageous conversations through a powerful combination of face-to-face training, online social-learning and individual experiences. We work with a wide range of organisations in health, education, housing, government and business. I'd love to hear about your experiences of courageous conversations, and what you would like to see included in the next edition of this book. If you want to get in touch, my email is larry@ccatwork.com. I look forward to hearing from you!

Larry Reynolds